E   A

P
I
A
N

S
E
A

③ PERSIA
became increasingly powerful under
Cyrus after 550; ruled the world
from S. Egypt to the Black Sea;
conquered from Greece by Alexander
the Great in 330 B.C.

•Cizre

Carchemish •Arslân-   •Haran
            Tash
                                    •Khorsabad
                          Nineveh •   •Arbela
•Aleppo   •Calah
                          A S S Y R I A

③   Ashur•   •Nuzi   ① ASSYRIA
①   expanded in 9th century B.C.;
                                                      overpowered Samaria in 721;
Hamath•   declined shortly after the   •Achmetha
②   defeat of Egypt in 660, and   Ecbatana
                                                      was destroyed by the
                                                      Babylonians in 612   •Bisutun
                •Mari   (Behistun)
                                                                                  P E R S I A
ascus   ② BABYLONIA   •Baghdad
                           became increasingly powerful after
                           625 B.C.; captured Jerusalem in   A C C A D
                           598 and destroyed it in 586,
                           sending the Jews into exile; was   •Babylon   •Susa
                           overthrown by the Persians in 538
   S Y R I A N   •Nippur
                                                              S U M E R
                                                         •Lagash
   D E S E R T   Erech•
                                                     •Larsa
                                                      •Ur

        0   50   100   150   200   250 miles

SHORTER ATLAS OF THE BIBLE

SHORTER ATLAS
OF THE BIBLE

LUC. H. GROLLENBERG

translated by
MARY F. HEDLUND, M.A. (OXON.)

NELSON
1965

THOMAS NELSON AND SONS LTD

36 Park Street London WI
Parkside Works Edinburgh 9
10 Warehouse Road Apapa Lagos
P.O. Box 25012 Nairobi

THOMAS NELSON (AUSTRALIA) LTD
597 Little Collins Street Melbourne CI

THOMAS NELSON AND SONS (SOUTH AFRICA) (Proprietary) LTD
P.O. Box 9881 Johannesburg

THOMAS NELSON AND SONS (CANADA) LTD
81 Curlew Drive Don Mills Ontario

THOMAS NELSON AND SONS
Copewood and Davis Streets Camden 3, N.J.

First published 1959
Reprinted 1961, 1965

Originally published as
KLEINE ATLAS VAN DE BIJBEL
(Amsterdam – Elsevier)

Foreword

This SHORTER ATLAS OF THE BIBLE is an attempt to present in small compass a picture of the world in which the books of the Bible found their origin. It is not simply a shortened version of the *Atlas of the Bible*. The material has been designed anew, on the same principles, using maps, a large number of illustrations, and a short text to link them; but it has been designed to suit the smaller format and to provide as much as possible for as low a price as possible. Naturally, this has meant some limitations.

First, the maps: these are confined to the key periods and show only the most important places. Those readers who seek more detailed information are referred to the larger Atlas, the Index of which contains virtually every geographical name in the Bible.

Again, the illustrations are fewer than in the larger work. Consequently, the selection has been to some extent revised, partly for didactic reasons, partly for reasons of printing technique, and finally because archaeologists have not been idle during the past four years and therefore something of their activities and discoveries had to be presented.

To make the best use of space and layout, the text is divided into short chapters of two to four pages, in which occasionally sketch maps and tables are inserted to clarify certain points. Brief references to relevant photographs in other parts of the book have been included. A further aim was to produce a pleasantly readable text. Lastly, the use of this Atlas in schools was considered, with the understanding that to the teacher would fall the lot of explaining more fully the unavoidably compressed accounts that are given.

What this SHORTER ATLAS OF THE BIBLE has to offer in the three fields of cartography, illustration, and text is naturally a limited selection from an abundance of material. That other selections were possible and equally to be defended, no one is more aware than the author himself. Often hesitating, he was helped to a decision by a deep conviction which, though it is nowhere explicitly formulated in the text, the reader is likely now and then to perceive. This is the conviction, first, that Israel alone of all the peoples of the world came in the course of the ages to an appreciation of God which implied a coherent interpretation of the mysteries of mankind; and, secondly, that the life, death, and resurrection of Jesus of Nazareth open the way for all men to a complete development of their human existence. The author has ventured to place before the public this attempt at a realistic approach to the lands of the Bible, in the hope that someone may by its means become more familiar with the Book of Books, and thus make his own something of that way of life which is able to make men happy.

Thanks are here expressed to the translator, Miss Hedlund, and to Fr. Mark Schoof O.P. for his careful and intelligent co-operation in the correction of the proofs.

LUC. GROLLENBERG O.P.

Jerusalem,
September 1959

CONTENTS

The Background

	Page	Map
A Strip of Land between Sea and Desert	9	
Endpaper Map: In the Heart of the Ancient World		Endpaper
Meeting Place of Many Cultures	15	
Reconnaissance in Palestine	25	
Map 1: Palestine: Geographical Survey showing the Most Important Excavations		facing p. 84
Remnants of Ancient Civilisations	31	
Excavation of Tells and Tombs	37	
Deciphering the Ancient Tongues	43	
The Technique of Biblical Geography	51	

The Old Testament

	Page	Map
The Chronicles of the Old Testament	57	
The Patriarchs	63	
Map 2: The Wanderings of the Patriarchs		84
Exodus from the House of Bondage	73	
Settlement in Canaan	79	
Map 3: Campaigns of Joshua and the Judges		85
From Joshua to Saul	85	
Jerusalem – City of David and of God	91	
Map 4: Jerusalem		85
Judah and Israel	99	
Map 5: From Saul to the Exile		100
In the Hands of the Assyrians	109	
Map 6: The Expansion of Assyria		101
The Prophets	115	
Exile and Return	123	
Map 7: The Persian Empire and Alexander the Great		101
The Jews in the Hellenistic World	129	

The New Testament

	Page	Map
Under the Roman Eagle	135	
Voices in the Wilderness	145	
The Hireling and the Good Shepherd	151	
The Gospels: Background and Composition	153	
Map 8: The Palestine of the Gospels and Acts		168
Jesus of Nazareth	159	
'My Witnesses to the End of the Earth'	169	
Map 9: The Travels of Saint Paul		169
Notes on the Plates	175	
Index	188	

Legend

The following abbreviations are used throughout for those books of the Bible which are referred to in the text and maps:

Old Testament

Gn	= Genesis
Ex	= Exodus
Lv	= Leviticus
Nu	= Numbers
Dt	= Deuteronomy
Jos	= Joshua
Jg	= Judges
2 S	= 2 Samuel
1 K, 2 K	= 1 and 2 Kings
1 Ch, 2 Ch	= 1 and 2 Chronicles
Ps	= Psalms
Pr	= Proverbs
Is	= Isaiah
Jer	= Jeremiah
Ezk	= Ezekiel
Dn	= Daniel
Am	= Amos
2 Mac	= 2 Maccabees

New Testament

Mt	= Matthew
Mk	= Mark
Lk	= Luke
Jn	= John
Ac	= Acts
Ro	= Romans
1 Co, 2 Co	= 1 and 2 Corinthians
Gal	= Galatians
Eph	= Ephesians
Ph	= Philippians
Col	= Colossians
1 and 2 Thess	= 1 and 2 Thessalonians
1 and 2 Ti	= 1 and 2 Timothy
Tit	= Titus
Philem	= Philemon
1, 2, 3 Jn	= 1, 2, and 3 John

The following references and abbreviations are used in the text:

p. 43	= see page 43
→36	= see the photograph on page 36
→84★	= see photograph on page 84 and additional information in the Notes on the Plates (pp. 175–186)
EP	= see the map on the front endpaper
ca	= circa
cf.	= compare
T.	= Tell

The spelling of Biblical names in this book is usually that of the Revised Standard Version of the Bible.

For Arabic names the English system of transliteration has been used.

Nihil Obstat:
Thomas Hanlon, L.S.S., S.T.L., Censor Deputatus
Die 14 Octobris 1959

Imprimatur:
+ Gordon Joseph, Archbishop of St Andrews and Edinburgh
Die 14 Octobris 1959

A STRIP OF LAND BETWEEN SEA AND DESERT

A nation's development is largely determined by the nature of the soil upon which it lives, the climate of its country, and the means of communication with other inhabited areas. The ancient nation of Israel was no exception to this rule. In so far as the Bible reflects the cultural and spiritual development of Israel, an intelligent understanding of the Bible demands some knowledge of geographical data. As far as Palestine is concerned these data are very interesting. The map of this land, so easy to draw with its simple lines of Jordan valley and coast, is reproduced on a small scale on the front endpaper of this atlas against the background of a much larger region which includes no less than five seas.

One should begin here by noting two things. The first is the character of the Syrian or Syro-Arabian desert east of Palestine, an endless, stony steppe, about 2,000 ft. above sea-level, where the rain from the west scarcely penetrates and where there are few oases. Until the advent of motorised transport this desert country made direct traffic between Palestine (with Egypt lying behind) and the region round the Persian Gulf impossible. Even for the camel, the one-humped species which came into use during the second millennium B.C., large sections of this steppe are scarcely passable, above all the basalt region southeast of Damascus (cf. the sketch on p. 15). For although the camel can go for days without water and store a provision of food in its hump which can, if necessary, be supplemented by dry grass and thistles, its hoofs are made for sandy ground and it moves with difficulty over rough stones and loose graved. The route from Jerusalem to Babylon, 537 miles apart as the crow flies, led first northeastwards, a long way pas Damascus, and then farther along the Euphrates in a southeasterly direction, a journey of roughly 780 miles. Cut off to the east by the Syrian Desert and west by a coast which offered little anchorage to sea traffic, Palestine could only be reached from the north and, less easily, from the south. This north south orientation is intensified by the second peculiarity revealed by the map and to which the attention of the reader is drawn. The map of Palestine is dominated by the vertical line of the Jordan valley which links two inland seas. This valley is considered the deepest in the world. The surface of the Sea of Galilee lies 700 ft. lower than the level of the Mediterranean Sea, that of the Dead Sea is 1290 ft. lower, and the bottom of the Dead Sea descends to 1311 ft. As a cross-section of Palestine at the level of Bethlehem shows (see p. 25), the surface of the desert appears to rise slightly and then suddenly dips down into the Jordan valley. It rises again to the west and then slopes gradually towards the coast. The relief of Palestine proper will be discussed later. Suffice it to remark here that this subsidence is not confined to Palestine. The sketch on the next page shows that it continues south of the Dead Sea in a 106 mile long valley, called in the Bible the Arabah, and is carried on near the small town of 'Aqaba, close to the ruins of the Biblical Elath, by a side-branch of the Red Sea. This valley also appears to continue north of Palestine. The map opposite suggests a similar sort of relief: the level of the desert first rises and forms Mount Hermon, continued north through the Anti-Lebanon; then follows a valley called the Beqaʿ (an Arabic word for valley), after which the level rises again to form the Lebanon. As can be seen on Map 2 (facing p. 84) the Orontes rises in the Beqaʿ and then flows northwards parallel to the coast. This points to a further continuation of the great north-south depression. Yet although this region resembles Palestine in the essential features of its ground relief, there are also considerable differences. The mountains on either side of the depression are very much higher. Moreover, the Beqaʿ, although it appears to be a continuation of the Jordan valley, is in reality separated from it by a piece of mountainous land. All these factors make it easy to understand how in antiquity the Lebanon and Palestine could be classed together under the name Canaan, while, on the other hand, the inhabitants of Palestine could at a certain period form a cultural and political unit.

The numbers on the map are those of the pages of photographs on which the regions mentioned are shown: in the north the old Phoenician trading city of Tripolis (→12*, top); in the background the snow-covered Lebanon (the root *lbn* means 'to be white'). To the south, where the plain narrows considerably between the mountains and the sea, is Byblos (→ 30). Then comes a view across the wide Beqaʿ to the majestic Hermon (→ 12, foot) whose name is derived from *hrm*, sacred, unassailable. Next follows a picture of the Sea of Galilee (→ 164–165) with Tiberias in the foreground and in the distance the Transjordan highlands. The photograph of the Jordan Valley (→ facing*), taken from a very great height in a north northwesterly direction, includes the lake in the hazy background, upper right. The dark ribbon running from there to the lower left is the dense undergrowth called in the Bible the 'pride' of the Jordan, inhabited in ancient times by so many animals that only the daring risked showing themselves there (cf. Jer 12 : 5). The rapidly flowing Jordan covers the 68 miles from the Sea of Galilee to the Dead Sea (→ 24) with so many twists and turns that its length is reckoned at 200 miles! Finally, there is an aerial photo of the Arabah (→ 28, foot) with the desolate landscape of the Negeb in the foreground and, across the valley, the highlands. There, in the dark strip, lie the ruins of the famous 'rose red' city of Petra (→ 138).

MEETING PLACE OF MANY CULTURES

Accessible only from the north and south the coastal region formed the natural link between the two most important cultural regions of antiquity, Egypt and Mesopotamia. According to the ancient Egyptians themselves, their land consisted of two parts (1 and 2 on the sketch below): the Nile valley proper, many hundreds of miles long and in most places 10 to 18 miles wide, flanked by sun-scorched deserts (→ 22, top★), and the broad fan-shaped Delta with sides of about 170 miles long. Agriculture depended entirely upon the annual flooding of the Nile, and only the well organised effort of all the inhabitants could turn it to advantage.

The earliest known Pharaoh, Menes, had already united the 'Two Lands' into one strong state. Both he and his earliest successors, who ruled from the magnificent and now completely vanished city of Memphis (→ 20–21★), just south of Cairo, and the later Pharaohs who had their court in Thebes, 375 miles to the south (→ 22, foot, 23★), wore a double crown, that of Upper and Lower Egypt. On the sides of their thrones especially they liked to have a symmetrical 'vignette' showing two Nile gods binding the papyrus reed of the Delta and the lotus of the Nile valley to the hieroglyph which expressed the concept of union (→ 50★). In the isolation of their country surrounded by desert, the Egyptians, conservative by nature, were able to preserve for three thousand years, without any essential changes, the first flowering of their astonishing culture. Their fertile soil, however, did not supply all their needs. They had no wood suitable for the building of houses and ships. From the very earliest times Egyptian traders sailed along the coast of Palestine to the Phoenician ports at the foot of the Lebanon, there to barter the products of their own country for lofty cedar trunks. In this way Byblos, for example, became almost an Egyptian city (→ 19★, 30, and p. 31). Later Pharaohs thought it worth while to undertake the wearying desert journey along the coast (106 miles from Pelusium to Raphia, see the map on p. 129) to occupy Canaan with

their armies and obtain the precious cedar wood by force (→ 13, 14★). Canaan had thus been in the power and under the influence of Egypt for some centuries before the Israelites settled there. As the latter expressed it, Canaan was a brother of Egypt and a son of Ham (cf. Gn 10 : 6). Their military expeditions sometimes carried the men of Thebes to the banks of the Euphrates, and every time they saw it they stood and stared. Here the world was completely topsy-turvy: a real river, almost as wide as their own Nile but flowing from north to south! Little did they realise that this 'backward-flowing' stream had, together with the Tigris, made possible the development of civilisations as least as old and as varied as their own, yet completely different.

Mesopotamia is also made up of two parts (3 and 4 on the sketch). The southern region is flat and can, if proper advantage be taken of the annual floods, be made extremely fertile. Here, shortly after 3000 B.C., flourished the Sumerian city states such as Ur, Lagash, and Nippur. North of the point where the two rivers are closest, where Baghdad now stands on the Tigris (see the front endpaper), with, 50 miles to the south, the ruins of Babylon near the Euphrates, the two rivers diverge and are separated by as much as 225 miles of steppe-like plains. The homeland of the Assyrians (near *a*) lay on the Tigris, between Cizre, where the river emerges from the upper region of the mountains (→ facing, foot*), and the two tributaries which are now called the Great and Little Zab. On the Euphrates, flowing far to the west, mighty cities and states flourished and decayed. Among them was Mari (→ facing, top*), 50 miles south of the place where the Khâbûr, the Habor of the Bible, flows into the Euphrates to the right of *b*.

Geographically, Mesopotamia was not nearly so isolated as Egypt. The two main rivers, much more capricious than the Nile, could suddenly overflow in southern Mesopotamia and sweep away the work of generations. It is not by chance that the earliest known version of the story of the Flood originated in this region. Sometimes, too, tribes from the northern highlands of Iran (5) and Armenia (6), and nomads from the Arabian peninsula, attracted by the riches of civilisation, poured into the regions along the Tigris and Euphrates and thus enriched the existing cultures with new elements. Whenever a power of any importance arose in Mesopotamia it automatically pressed westwards, where the Euphrates is no more than 125 miles from the coast, which can then be gained fairly easily. For this region (around 7 on the map), roughly corresponding to the modern states of Syria and Lebanon, was particularly attractive to Mesopotamian powers, not only as a jumping-off ground for expansion towards wealthy Egypt, not only on account of the fertile hinterland and the cedars of Lebanon, but also because of the Phoenician trading centres on the sea coast with its many bays. On Map 2 (facing p. 84) some of these trading centres are shown: the great city of Ugarit, destroyed *ca* 1200 B.C. by the so-called Peoples of the Sea and accidentally discovered in 1927 in the mound of *Râs Shamra*. Excavation of this *tell* still continues to provide valuable information concerning the ancient culture of Canaan. There was also the island city of Arvad (→ 18, top), the already mentioned towns of Tripolis and Byblos, Sidon, and finally Tyre (→ 18, foot). From the very earliest times the seafaring inhabitants of these cities carried on commercial relations with the western world, with the copper island of Cyprus, with the coasts of Asia Minor, and with the Greek archipelago, If one bears in mind that the northern part of the coastal region was strongly influenced by the Hittites of Asia Minor (8) it is obvious that one may indeed justifiably speak of this land as a meeting place of many cultures.

22

RECONNAISSANCE IN PALESTINE

The large map on the front endpaper shows a bird's eye view of Palestine, lying between five seas and on the only passable road linking Africa and Asia. On Map 1 (facing p. 84), we see the country on a larger scale. It is divided into two unequal parts by a green strip-the deep valley through which the Jordan flows to the Dead Sea, the most remarkable of all lakes (→ facing★). Here are a few short remarks concerning the country west of the Jordan valley. The colours show that the central chain of hills in the southern part, roughly between Hebron and Baal-hazor, is fairly high and massive (cf. the section below, level with Bethlehem; the sketch of the earth layers suggests that the region round the Dead Sea in particular is a paradise for geologists!). Farther north, where the central chain of mountains formerly bore the name of Ephraim, it descends and is often broken up by valleys. Near Shechem it is even transversed by a narrow cleft. The mountain to the south was called Mount Gerizim, that to the north Mount Ebal, and between these two massive peaks lay ancient Shechem (→ 68–69★). Alongside the two mountains, on the eastern side, lies a narrow fertile plain which, when our photograph was taken, at the beginning of June, was 'white for harvest' (→ 67, foot★). A little farther, past ancient Tirzah, after which a wide vale opens on to the valley of the Jordan (→ 105, top), the mountain country seems to divide: one half runs northwest, ending in Mount Carmel which descends steeply into the sea (→ 119), the other northeast, where the crescent-shaped mountain barrier of Gilboa bounds the plain of Jezreel (→ 89, foot★). From Megiddo one looks across the plain to where the central mountain range begins again in Lower Galilee (→ 84 top, cf. → 27 foot, from the top of Mount Tabor). There lies Nazareth and, a little farther north, *Kafr Kenna* (→ 27, top).

The coastal plain, protected over most of its length by a line of dunes, is very broad in the south where once the Philistines lived. After Joppa (Jaffa) comes the much narrower plain of Sharon, marshy, since the dunes prevent the water from draining off, and mentioned in the Bible for its impenetrable and luxuriant vegetation. On the right-hand side of Map 1, one sees how the highlands east of the Jordan valley are divided into four by the deep clefts of the Yarmuk (not mentioned in the Bible), the Jabbok (→ 65 foot, cf. 11★), and the Arnon (→ 78, top).

After this rapid glance at the ground relief, two other closely related factors must be taken into consideration: the rainfall distribution and the position of the natural trade routes. During the summer, from mid-May until mid September there is no rain at all in Palestine. The dew, however, is sometimes very heavy and of real importance for agriculture. The rainfall during the remaining months, of which the first and last showers ('the early and later rains', Dt 11 : 14, etc.) are so indispensable for good harvests, comes from above the Mediterranean and is naturally heavier in the northern part of Palestine than in the south, where the coastline begins to curve towards the west. In addition, the central mountain chain attracts most rain where it is highest. This means that the mountains of Judaea and also the hills to the west (called by the Judaeans the Lowland) catch most of the rain, while the east side, the Wilderness of Judaea ($\rightarrow$ 29*), lies within the 'rain shadow' and receives very little. The same is true of the deep and tropically hot Jordan valley. Towards the north, where the mountain chain becomes lower and more broken up, the rain can penetrate farther east. This part of the Jordan valley is thus better suited for agriculture, since it also possesses many springs and brooklets. The steeply rising edge of the district east of the Jordan receives a heavier precipitation throughout its entire length.

The route followed by the main roads is also determined by the relief of the country. As can be seen from the dotted lines on Map 1 (facing p. 84), only two main traffic roads are possible in the south, both running north to south, one along the coast and the other along the central mountain chain. Quite a number of Israelite cities lay along this road, and the modern asphalt road from Hebron to Shechem follows the same route. Anyone driving reflectively along it on a clear day can see on his left the Mediterranean sparkling behind the coastal plain with its row of dunes, and on his right the edge of the Transjordan highland. If he takes the trouble to climb a high peak, like *Nebi Samwîl* near Gibeon ($\rightarrow$ 82, centre*) he will be able to see both boundaries and marvel at the wonderful structure of this Holy Land.

Past Shechem the situation becomes less easy to survey. The plain of Jezreel, joining the coastal plain in the northwest at the bay of Acco and running east to Beth-shan, offers here the only possibility of easy communication between east and west. In addition, the bulk of Mount Carmel forces the coastal road (the main road from Egypt to Mesopotamia!) to curve in a northeasterly direction, through the pass which emerges on to the plain near Megiddo and there to cross the road running from west to east.

This rapid survey makes it clear how much the situation of the northern tribes of Israel differed from that of the tribe of Judah, who lived rather isolated in their hilly ($\rightarrow$ 28, top), yet compact and clearly defined highland. It was not by chance that four successive kings had their capitals here, at Shechem, Penuel, Tirzah and Samaria. Life was easier for the northern Israelites in their more fertile and well-watered land. They mingled unobtrusively with the Canaanites who had stayed on the fertile plains of Jezreel, Acco, and Beth-shan, and had varied contacts with the Phoenicians of Tyre and Sidon and the Aramaic states in the northeast. In this flourishing, open country they were perhaps an easy prey for pagan conquest and influence. On the other hand, their descendants in Jesus' time were readier to accept His preaching of the Kingdom.

REMNANTS OF ANCIENT CIVILISATIONS

The entire region so far discussed, that is Palestine, Syria, and Egypt on the one hand, and Mesopotamia on the other, is studded with ruins from the past. Some still rise high above the landscape, others have been buried for centuries beneath sand and silt. The ancient Egyptians built their simple houses of mud bricks (→ 75), not a very durable material. For this reason scarcely anything remains of great cities like Memphis, and palms now grow where houses once stood (→ 20–21). But for their 'eternal homes', as they called their tombs, and for the temples of their gods, they used either blocks of natural stone, found in abundance in the desert on either side of their land, or else hard granite from Elephantine (→ 131, foot) and regions farther south. This they fashioned and transported with the most amazing skill. The fact that they used this stone accounts for the numerous visible ruins in Egypt. Admittedly they were often partly buried during the course of time under Nile silt and drifting sand (see for example the difference in colour on the pillars at Luxor, → 71), but this helped to preserve many precious reliefs, like those on top of a fallen obelisk in Karnak (→ 42), and even whole buildings, like the magnificent temple at Edfu (→ 132, foot).

In Mesopotamia, however, there was scarcely any stone suitable for building. The inhabitants mostly used bricks baked in the sun or in a fire, with bitumen for mortar (Gn 11 : 3). Centuries of rain storms and floods reduced these ancient cities to shapeless heaps of clay. Only the remains of the temple towers (called ziggurats) still rise here and there above the wide plain. These were enormous constructions which the people built in order to draw closer to the gods, or rather, to offer the gods a ladder down which they could climb to the earth (→ 61, foot*).

Syria and Palestine contain ruins of all kinds and of every century. Sometimes a whole series of successive cultures is represented on one spot. One example is Byblos, shown opposite. In the foreground is the Mediterranean Sea; behind the narrow, fertile coastal plain is the beginning of the Lebanon flank which rises to about 9,000 ft. above sea-level. The village to the left is called *Jebeil* and thus retains the old name which the Assyrians spelled Gubla and the Israelites Gebal. The inhabitants were known as wood-workers (1 K 5 : 18) and shipbuilders (Ezk 27 : 9). This is understandable as they had little space for agriculture or cattle breeding but had immense cedar woods behind them and a coast with many sheltered bays in front of them. The church in the centre of the village (in circle 1) was built by the Crusaders who occupied Giblet, as they called it, from 1104 to 1188, and after that from 1198 until a stormy night in 1266, when the last defenders escaped from the superior besiegers of Sultan Baibars across the sea to Tripolis. The church, with its magnificent baptistery, is in pure Romanesque style. The fort, of which the keep can be seen (in circle 2), dates from the same period. The amphitheatre (in circle 3) is Roman and fully a thousand years older. At this time the slopes of the Lebanon were already largely denuded of their cedars, but Byblos, as it was pronounced in those days, continued to flourish thanks to the cult of Adonis whose myth was localised in the neighbourhood. Two thousand years older again than the amphitheatre is the temple (in circle 4) with its many obelisks (close-up view → 19).

As early as 3000 B.C. Egyptian merchants visited this town, already famous as a religious centre, and incorporated it into their legends about Isis and Osiris. Yet what they were really seeking in this land of gods was cedar wood. They received the precious trunks mainly in exchange for the writing material which they made from the papyrus reeds of their Delta. The Greek world obtained these sheets of papyrus from Byblos and it was thus that a book, in Greek, came to be called *biblion* from which is derived, via the Latin *biblia*, our word *Bible*, the book par excellence. The Greeks also adopted the writing system of the Phoenicians who, after centuries of experiment (the development is not yet completely clear), had succeeded, long before 1000 B.C., in simplifying the old complicated method of writing into an alphabet. To the right of the house in the foreground, used by the excavators as a workshop and storage place, one can see the foundations of houses built *ca* 4000 B.C. Counting from the medieval church and fort, this photo thus shows remains dating over a period of more than fifty centuries. One must bear in mind that the Roman amphitheatre was only revealed by excavation; it even owes its present site to the diggers who moved it because they wanted to continue excavating the original site. The same is true of the temple in 4. All these investigations were possible because the village of Jebeil and the Giblet of the Crusaders were built beside the ruins of ancient Gubla/Byblos and not on top of them.

Happily for the archaeologists this also happened in other places, such as the town of Hama on the Orontes (→ facing, top) picturesquely situated about the tell of the ancient city which appears in the Bible as Hamath. This tell is so high that it rises above the white domes of the buildings and the musically creaking paddle-wheels which convey part of the river water to high aqueducts (→ facing, foot). The height of the tell is due to the fact that Hamath was destroyed and rebuilt many times.

The houses in these regions were not very solidly built. The walls were usually made of two rows of rough stones. The cavity was filled with pebbles and the outside smeared with mud. Sometimes the upper part of the wall was made of bricks of sun-baked clay. The flat roof rested on light beams and more earth was smeared on top. When a town was destroyed only the lower part of the walls remained standing; the spaces in between became filled up with the materials of the upper structure. The inhabitants, those who had not been put to the sword or died of plague or starvation, departed. Wind and rain flattened everything to a mound of earth. Such a mound was already called a *tell* in the oldest Semitic languages. Drawn by the attractive site people then came years later to live on this spot. As Jeremiah expressed it 'the city shall be rebuilt on its mound' (Jer 30 : 18). With every succeeding destruction the mound rose higher. Turning now from the tell of Hama, the following chapter will deal with the investigation of tells in Palestine.

EXCAVATION OF TELLS AND TOMBS

Where a tell consists of the accumulated remains of successively destroyed cities, the walls of a trench dug down through this mound should show as many layers as there were cities. Oddly enough, this simple principle was only discovered in 1890, although scholars had already been engaged for half a century in investigating the antiquities of Palestine. They had completely overlooked the numerous tells. In that year W. Flinders Petrie set out to examine a tell in the land of the Bible. Throughout the preceding ten years this young Englishman had rendered great service to archaeology by his meticulous examination of tells in the Nile Delta. He had, among other things, learned to appreciate the true importance of such apparent trifles as potsherds. In 1890 he dug a number of trenches through *Tell el-Hesy*, east of Gaza (for this and other place names see the folding Map 1, facing p. 84). He immediately distinguished a number of layers, noted that each contained its characteristic shards, and could even assign an approximate date to some of them, since they yielded objects which he was able to fit into the already established periods of ancient Egyptian history. In this manner Petrie laid the foundations for a completely new and very important development in Palestinian archaeology.

During the years that followed, up to the First World War, a number of other tells were investigated, those of Gezer, Gaza, Taanach, Megiddo, Samaria, and Jericho, by archaeological societies of various countries. After the war, when Palestine had become British mandated territory, a second phase began. Many countries took part under the supervision of the excellent Department of Antiquities and worked in close contact with each other. This contact was made easier by the newly created road network. National unrest, followed by the Second World War brought archaeological activity almost to a standstill. Now, we have entered upon the third phase, but in a land divided. The Archaeological Service of Israel is extremely active, not only in important undertakings, such as that at Hazor (→ 83*) but also in numerous other places where digging during the course of house and road building has turned up interesting relics of the past. In Jordan all possible facilities have been afforded foreign teams. During the past few years excavations have been made at Dothan (→ 35*), Shechem (→ 68–69), Tirzah (→ 105, top* and facing*), Jericho, *Khirbet Qumrân* (→ 142), and in Transjordan at Dibon.

The ideal method of investigating a tell is, of course, to begin by completely uncovering the remains of the most recent city. These are removed in their turn and the remains of the preceding city are examined. This process is continued until the foundations of the earliest city are laid bare. Such a method, however, is usually far too costly. For although ancient cities were usually small in size, the uncovering of such an area requires a large number of labourers who, under the leadership of experienced foremen, would allow no detail to escape them. It also requires a trained staff of surveyors, photographers, and draughtsmen to record accurately any finds made. For, before proceeding to the following layer the first must be removed, and with it all the evidence. It is thus imperative that a record should be made for scientific publications in which later generations may find every detail of the original situation, since destroyed. It is for this reason that archaeologists usually confine themselves to a partial excavation. Once a tell has been selected (not only historical but practical considerations play a rôle here – ease of access, water supply, the proximity of a village which can supply diggers, etc.) a trial ditch is usually dug at the edge of the tell (see our aerial photo of Dothan, → 35, taken in 1953 during the first campaign) and a spot is chosen which seems likely to yield something of particular interest, a city gate, a palace, or a temple. If more money can be raised for the actual excavation and for scientific publications besides those concerning the work in progress (anyone who obtains a licence to dig must undertake to publish a record of his finds), a new section can be broached (→ 83, top★).

Since Petrie's time and especially in the second period, the technique of exposing the layers and interpreting their contents has progressed considerably. This can be attributed in part to an increasingly accurate knowledge of the shapes and workmanship of the pottery made during the various periods of antiquity. The study of this pottery is of the greatest importance for dating a layer which is being excavated, and nowadays an experienced archaeologist is able to assess the age of a small fragment to within a few centuries and that of a complete article to within a century. Along with a few typical pots and jars the page facing shows a series of oil lamps of which the upper one dates from 2000 B.C. and the four below from the Graeco-Roman period.

Anyone excavating a tell always searches eagerly for the necropolis, the place or places in which the former inhabitants buried their dead. In the countries around Palestine the burial sites, at least those of any importance, were always indicated by a stone superstructure resembling those in Egypt (pyramids, mastabas), in some regions of Phoenicia (→ 40 top★), and in Petra (→ 138, top★). The ancient inhabitants of Palestine usually buried their dead in the natural caves in which their hilly country abounds, or hewed burial chambers from the soft sandstone. Those tombs which have remained intact are exceedingly difficult to find (otherwise they would have either been plundered or cleared for further use) and testify to a high level of culture so far as one can judge from the funeral gifts. These finds vary enormously (→ 41★). In the Museum voor Oudheden in Leiden one may admire the contents of a rock tomb from Jericho dating from 1700 B.C. Everything is laid out exactly as it was found (→ 40, foot).

Teams of scholars from many countries, continually reinforced by enthusiastic young assistants, are collaborating in the examination of the land of Palestine. They are supported financially either by their own government or by some archaeological institution. In this manner we obtain each year a clearer picture of the daily life of the Israelites throughout the various periods of their history and also of that of their predecessors in this land, as far back as the prehistoric cave-dwellers.

DECIPHERING THE ANCIENT TONGUES

The examination of the ruins scattered about Egypt, Mesopotamia, and the Syria-Palestine coastal region would offer us no coherent picture of the early history of these lands if we were unable to read the texts found there. Happily we are able to do so thanks to some remarkable feats of linguistic skill, ranking with the greatest inventions of modern times.

Up to the beginning of the 19th century Egyptian hieroglyphs remained a mystery, although this puzzling writing was familiar enough. Since imperial times Rome had possessed a number of obelisks, enormous square columns with a pyramid-shaped top, always hewn from a single block. Some of these proud trophies from the land of the Pharaohs, where such pillars used to flank the temple doors, were covered on every side with hieroglyphs. In 1831 an obelisk was erected in Paris as a present from Mohamed Ali to the French king Louis-Philippe. As one can read on the base of this obelisk, in the Place de la Concorde, the civil engineer who arranged the transport was very pleased with the success of his undertaking. He did not know, apparently, that around 660 B.C. the Assyrians had conveyed two such obelisks from Thebes to Nineveh, a much longer and more difficult journey!

J. F. Champollion (1790–1832), who as a boy had listened breathlessly to stories of Napoleon's expedition in Egypt, felt it his vocation to resolve the mystery of the hieroglyphs. To this end he studied Chinese, Arabic, Hebrew, Syriac and above all Coptic, the language of the Egyptian Christians, and the only living link with the past. After fifteen years of dogged searching he found the first clue in 1822 and on his death, at the age of 42, he left behind him a grammar of ancient Egyptian in manuscript form. After him a number of able Egyptologists penetrated further into the mysteries of this language and from the numerous texts reconstructed the history of the ancient Egyptians and their admirable culture.

Hieroglyphic writing consists of symbols depicting physical objects, and in the earliest examples these symbols were carved in stone. When writing on papyrus became widely practised their form was simplified to the 'hieratic' or sacred script, used by the priests, and then further simplified for business or popular use to the 'demotic' or people's script. In this last the pictorial element was entirely lost. At first the symbols were direct drawings of things, but the system became more useful when the same drawings were used not only for the actual objects depicted, but also for things or abstract ideas which had the same sounds as these objects. Thus in reading hieroglyphic writing we must pay attention both to the objects depicted by the symbols and to their sounds.

On the opposite page is shown one side of the pyramid-shaped top of a fallen and broken obelisk in Thebes which was 96½ ft. high and weighed 325 tons. Without Champollion we could have admired the splendid composition of the figures, evidently a god extending his hands in blessing over a kneeling king, but would have understood nothing more of the meaning. Now we can read the signs, starting at the upper right column: 'Words spoken by Amon-Re, lord of the heavens: I have given [2nd column] the rule of the Two Lands entirely to my daughter [3rd column, the name is outlined in a *cartouche*] Maat-ka-Re as she desires. May she live!' This Maat-ka-Re, 'righteousness is the essence of (the Sun-god) Re', is known as the only woman Pharaoh of importance, usually known by her maiden name of Hatshepsut, 'pinnacle of noble women' and famed for the magnificent temple of the dead which she had built against the steep rock wall guarding the Valley of the Kings (→ 23, foot). After a reign of twenty years this queen was forcibly deposed *ca* 1480 B.C. by her half-brother and husband, Thothmes III, who had her statues everywhere torn down and her name effaced. The top of our obelisk happily survived this destruction but was, however, the victim of another. On the photo one can plainly see that the figure of the god Amon with his tall feathers lies deeper in the stone than that of the queen, depicted as a man; the same is true of the hieroglyphs in the right-hand column giving his name and title, 'lord of heaven'. In roughly 1377 B.C. Amenophis IV came to the throne. He wished the solar disk, Aton, to be the only god venerated. His fanaticism drove him to have the name of the supreme god Amon everywhere effaced. The zealous servants of Akhenaton ('it is pleasing to Aton'), as he called himself, even cimbed the tall obelisk of Hatshepsut to cut away Amon's name and title. This religious reformer, who had built a brand-new capital exactly between Memphis and Thebes, near the modern el-Amarna, died *ca* 1358 B.C. misunderstood by his people and leaving the state in chaos. Then the priests of Amon set about rectifying the wrong done to their god and restored his name and images as well as they could, as we see here on our obelisk. The traces of the restoration, however, have remained visible. From this example one sees that now, due to the work of Champollion and his successors, the dead stones of Egypt speak to us.

Eloquent, too, are numerous papyri, covered with writing, which survived in this rainless land. At the very beginning of their history, around 3000 B.C., the Egyptians evolved a method of making writing material from the papyrus reeds which grew in the Nile Delta. Long strips of reed were laid side by side to the required width and another layer of shorter strips was placed across them at right angles. These two layers were then soaked in water, pressed, and left to dry in the sun. The resulting sheets were joined together into a long roll on which marks could be traced with the aid of ink and thin styluses. These signs were also hieroglyphs, but in the cursive form which is called hieratic script.

Sometimes drawings were added, often in colour and as carefully drawn as the best medieval miniatures. Many such drawings are found in the collection of texts which, after 1600 B.C., used to be buried with embalmed dead and which is usually known as the Book of the Dead. Our photograph of a vignette from the copy in the Museum voor Oudheden in Leiden (which also possesses the writers' palettes shown below, → 55*) shows Osiris, the god of the dead, in his chapel. Before him stands Maat, goddess of justice, and in front of her the god Thoth, who supervises Horus' manipulation of the scales. Upon these scales the heart of the dead person, in this case a woman who looks on in suspense, is being weighed against justice, in the form of a miniature statue of Maat. Under the scales lies a monster of hell. Besides all sorts of magic formulae the Book of the Dead also contains speeches like the following, which the deceased had to pronounce before his heavenly judge: 'I have done no wrong, I have not robbed, I have not been covetous, I have not stolen, I have killed no man, I have not given short measure of corn . . .' And more positive: 'I have done what is pleasing to the gods, I have given bread to the hungry and water to the thirsty and clothes to the naked and a passage to those with no boat . . .'

In Mesopotamia there were no papyrus plants. In ancient times the southern part was one of the most fertile regions in the world, since the soil was composed entirely of thick river clay. In the 4th millennium before Christ the Sumerians had already discovered that a mark scratched on a flattened lump of clay was ineffaceable once the clay had hardened in the sun, and also that drawings could serve to depict ideas and messages. Soon they began to stylise their drawings of all sorts of objects. The stylus left a thicker impression where it was first pressed on the clay, making the signs wedge-shaped (Lat. *cuneus*, 'wedge', hence the term cuneiform writing). This stylisation soon made the original object unrecognisable, while other signs were added in order to express more elements of the language unambiguously. When the country of the Sumerians was occupied by the Accadians, *ca* 2250 B.C., the latter used the cuneiform writing for their own Semitic language. Many signs were given different meanings and sound values and new signs were added. This process continued throughout the turbulent history of Mesopotamia and in the meantime cuneiform writing came to be used outside this region. In a study of the evolution of cuneiform writing which appeared in 1926 35,438 different signs were recorded.

Happily for us, the Elamites, who lived in the mountainous country north of ancient Sumer, also adopted the system and greatly simplified it, leaving only 113 syllabic signs. The Persians further reduced these to 41. The enthralling history of the decipherment of this language begins indeed with texts which travellers had copied in Persepolis, the 'City of the Persians'. There were found inscriptions which, as later appeared, rendered the same text in three different languages, Persian, Elamite, and Babylonian. In 1802 the German teacher Grotefend very keenly observed that in what was apparently the simplest section occurred the names of the Persian kings Hystaspes, Darius, and Xerxes; this gave him the equivalent of thirteen letters. An English Indian army officer, Rawlinson, very interested in the deciphering work, succeeded after superhuman efforts in making a copy of the enormous inscription which Darius (522–486) had had carved on the steep rock-face of Bisutun (Behistun). There, 390 ft. above the ground, stood a lengthy text, in the three above-mentioned languages and scripts. The deciphering of the third, which contained the largest number of different signs, was made easier by the collaboration of many scholars and by the influx of reliefs from the Assyrian towns which being excavated at this time, in which the meaning of the inscriptions was often made clear by the pictures. In 1848 the Royal Asiatic Society gave a text to four experts-Rawlinson, Talbot, an Irish priest, and a

German, and asked them to translate it independently of each other. The four results were identical in all essential points and the gateway to Mesopotamian antiquity was open at last. Since this time scholars have assiduously studied the refinements of the Babylonic-Assyrian language in every phase of its development and with the knowledge obtained have conquered other domains, that of the Sumerian language and culture, for example, and the completely forgotten world of the Hittites in Asia-Minor.

In this limited space it has only been possible to show a few specimens of the very considerable number of cuneiform documents: the Legal Code of king Hammurabi of Babylon (*ca* 1728–1686, → 47*), engraved upon stone, and a few texts on clay (→ 48*). The deciphering of a great number of documents has made it possible to establish a chronology and thus to reconstruct ancient history. In this the lists of kings found in several towns of Mesopotamia have proved of immeasurable value. These lists gave the names of a number of successive rulers of a city or state with the length of their reign. Important events were dated according to the year of the ruler's reign, and also eclipses of the sun and moon. A number of definite facts could thus be determined with the help of modern astronomy. There were also texts referring to campaigns against and treaties with other countries in which kings mentioned the names of their foreign colleagues.

There is unfortunately no space to give a large table of ancient eastern history similar to that given on page 116. It would have to begin with the year 3000 B.C. and give on the left the history of Egypt in its four periods: the Old Kingdom (2850–2050), the Middle Kingdom (2050–1780), the New Kingdom (1610–715), and the Later Period (715–332), while the right-hand side would show the principal dynasties and kingdoms of Mesopotamia. In the centre, roughly between 1650 and 1200 B.C., would stand the mighty kingdom of the Hittites and beside it, between 1460 and 1300, the buffer state of Mitanni in the Khâbûr region. It would then be obvious at a glance that Israel as a state, i.e. under David, only entered the scene comparatively late, *ca* 1000 B.C. This fact is extremely important, for the decipherment has revealed to us not only the history but also the culture of the nations before Israel, in many of its religious and social expressions.

In a good bookshop anyone can now buy large works containing translations of ancient eastern texts which in one way or another are of importance for the study of the Old Testament. Besides historical texts one finds accounts of the Creation and prehistorical events, all sorts of epics and myths, prayers, and songs of praise, love songs, proverbs full of worldly wisdom, philosophical works, prophecies and oracles, liturgical instructions, legal codes of every kind, letters, and so on, all translated from the languages which were used in Egypt, Mesopotamia, Syria, Palestine, and the land adjoining. A first acquaintance with these texts causes many to exclaim: 'these people feel and speak as they do in the Bible!' A closer examination of these mainly pre-Israelite texts leads one to say that Israel was indeed completely a product of its environment. And yet Israel possessed a quality inalienably its own, a quality which was never so obvious as in our day, thanks to the revelation of the Eastern past.

THE TECHNIQUE OF
BIBLICAL GEOGRAPHY

Early one morning in March 1928 a Syrian farmer was ploughing his strip of land near the Mediterranean Sea, close to the chalky and sometimes steep wall of a bay which his fellow-countrymen called *Minet el-Beida*, 'the white harbour'. Suddenly his primitive plough struck a heavy stone. When he had finally succeeded in lifting it he saw that it was the key-stone of a vault; the space beneath was a burial chamber full of inviting objects. It was then that the man did something for which archaeologists and Biblical scholars will always be grateful. He resisted the temptation to sell the dishes and jewellery for a good price in the antique market and reported his find to the authorities, at that time French. Archaeologists examined the tomb and its surroundings and then devoted their attention to the extensive tell lying half a mile inland. This was called *Râs Shamra*, 'hill of fennel', apparently because it was covered with this plant. A trial trench proved promising and it was decided to excavate. In the very first campaign, in 1929, on the highest part of the hill, spectacular finds were made, including a temple and a library containing numerous clay tablets covered with an unfamiliar kind of cuneiform writing. An old Phoenician trading city, of which Minet-el-Beida had apparently been the harbour, thus lay farther north than had ever been supposed. The scholars racked their brains to discover the name of this city. Could this be Zemar, already mentioned in Egyptian texts from the time of Thothmes III as a strong coastal city of Canaan and whose inhabitants, the Zemarites, are mentioned in the Bible after those of the island city of Arvad (Gn 10 : 18)? During the first campaign a stele (an upright memorial stone) was found (→ see 53, foot*), dedicated by an Egyptian official to the god Set of Saphon, a common city name also occuring in ancient Palestine as Zaphon (Jos 13 : 27). Could this have been the name of the city? No, said other scholars; for in the state archives of the Pharaohs Amenophis III and IV, which the latter had had transferred to his new capital near el-Amarna (see p. 44), and whose correspondence with the rulers of Asia (377 clay tablets or fragments) has cast so much light upon the situation in Canaan *ca* 1400 1370 B.C., an important rôle is played by Ugarit, a town which certainly lay far to the north. This must be Râs Shamra. These scholars proved to be right. When the new cuneiform writing (an alphabet of 29 letters) had been deciphered in an incredibly short time, the texts showed that the excavated city was indeed identical with Ugarit.

Anyone who studies Biblical geography meets the same sort of problem. On the one hand he has a number of texts at his disposal, beginning with the Bible itself. In the historical books especially many place names occur, usually in the narratives, occasionally in primarily geographical texts like Genesis 10 and above all Joshua 13–21. In addition he has non-Biblical texts, both ancient (for example the lists of conquered regions and cities of Asia which the Pharaohs, beginning with

Thothmes III, had carved on the walls of their temples and the bases of their statues (→ 50*) and the accounts of the campaigns of the Assyrian kings, etc.), and more recent (the Graeco-Roman writers, the Biblical-geographical works of Eusebius, Jerome, Arabian, medieval, and later scholars). On the other hand the Biblical geographer has the land before him as it is now, with its towns and villages and innumerable ruins and tells, whether he lives there (which is preferable) or possesses very good maps of the region. His problem is to identify the towns named in the Bible and to place them, as far as he can, in the correct locality. This is not always an easy task. If a place mentioned in the Bible is still inhabited under the same name, like Jerusalem, Bethlehem, Heshbon, etc. its identification presents no problem, nor is there any difficulty when the name of the old city is still clearly recognisable in that of its tell or of a place in the immediate neighbourhood, whether inhabited or not. *Tell Ta'annak* cannot be anything but the tell of the Biblical Taanach, near which Barak gave battle (Jg 5 : 19). The enormous *Tell el-Hosn* must contain the ruins of Biblical Beth-shan, for until 1949 the village of *Beisân*, an Arabic version of the old name, lay close by.

But where the old names have been forgotten and long since replaced by new ones; or where they have been so drastically corrupted as to be unrecognisable in the modern Arabic name for the tell or village, then the archaeologist and geographer must look elsewhere for evidence of identification. In earlier Biblical atlases one finds the town of Lachish indicated on the site of *Tell el-Hesy* (cf. p. 37); *Tell ed-Duweir*, 'the tell of the small monastery', 7½ miles farther east, appeared, however, to correspond more with the literary data. The excavations there (1933–37), in which the famous potsherds covered with writing were found (→ 54, top*), made identification with Lachish almost certain. Later atlases now reserve *Tell el-Hesy* for the Biblical Eglon, but with a large query. Here is yet another example. According to the ancient texts the Philistine town of Ekron must have stood where the coastal plain merges into the hill country, roughly parallel with Jerusalem. There, indeed, roughly 9 miles from the coast, one finds a village called '*Aqir*, apparently a derivation of Ekr(on). Many atlases thus situated the Biblical city there, but tentatively, for no shards of the Biblical period had been found either in or near the village. Israelite scholars have recently investigated the ruin *el-Muqanna'*, about 4½ miles farther south, and made its identification with Ekron extremely probable. This ruin, however, was considered by many to be the remains of the Biblical Eltekeh, for which another site must now be sought. Biblical Gibeon was usually seen in the village of *el-Jîb*, 6 miles northwest of old. Jerusalem (→ 82, centre*). Serious objections were however raised against this identification, disputing both the identity of the names and the conformity with the literary data. In the summer of 1956 the American, Pritchard, began a small excavation on this spot. He discovered an enormous round well, 36 ft. in diameter, hewn out of the rock, with steps running down the side (→ 81). This must have been the pool of Gibeon (2 S 2 : 13). The soil with which it was filled contained a large number of shards and wine jar handles and even funnels, and on 27 of the jar handles was the name Gibeon (→ opposite, top*). For the first time in 66 years of excavation a Palestinian ruin provided its own visiting-cards!

THE CHRONICLES OF THE
OLD TESTAMENT

Until late into the Middle Ages Jews and Christians were of the opinion that the first five books of the Bible were written by Moses himself. This great work, known as 'the Law' or, following an old Greek expression 'the Pentateuch' (the work 'composed of five scrolls'), was inseparably linked with the founder of Israel's religion. It dealt precisely with events from the creation of the world up to and including the mighty happenings on which the religion of Israel throughout the centuries that followed was to be based: the journey out of Egypt to freedom, the Covenant on Mount Sinai, and the journey to the Promised Land. Here Moses himself had played the leading rôle and all that he recorded concerning former times he could know by tradition. Could he not trace his descent back to Adam? It was even assumed that this greatest of all prophets, having learned the facts concerning the creation (Gn 1) had completed the work with the story of his own end (Dt 34: 1–8). Only in the Renaissance did men begin to doubt the truth of this age-old tradition. This was not so much because people at this time were distrustful of any kind of tradition. The Pentateuch, like other old writings, had now begun to be read in the original Hebrew. This was rendered possible for many by the distribution of printed Bibles in Hebrew, and now more attention was paid than in previous centuries to the literary qualities of this work.

It was soon discovered that the 'Law of Moses' contained many differences in style, repetitions, and contradictions which seemed to make the hypothesis of one author unlikely. Some also argued that at the time of Moses writing had either not been discovered or was still so primitive that such a varied and, in some parts, highly skilled literary work could not possibly have been written. That this last argument no longer holds water needs no further demonstration after the exposition on pages 43–46. As a reminder the opposite page shows the charming statuette of an Egyptian writer who lived 1000 years before Moses and who could afford this immortalisation thanks to the career he had made for himself after a lengthy schooling and the zealous study of a literature which by this time was already regarded as classical.

If Moses was really trained for a high office at the Pharaoh's court in the eastern Delta around 1300 B.C. he was probably familiar, not only with the Egyptian writing but also with the cuneiform script used for diplomatic correspondence with Asia. This means that, technically speaking, he was quite capable of writing an extensive work like the Pentateuch. In actual fact, however, this work was written centuries after his death. It is generally assumed that the text as we know it only came into existence in the 5th century B.C. At this period learned priests – after the Exile it was they who led the people – collected all kinds of story series and compilations of laws dating from former centuries and amplified them with material conserved in their own circles. All this they transformed into one whole in the manner which seemed to them best for the Jewish community. This process is indicated on the diagram on the left: oral traditions from the 'Hebrew' period I, laid down in various collections during the 'Israelite' period II, were expanded into the Pentateuch (A) of our Bible during the 'Jewish' period III. One should also note the position of the two other great historical works. The books of Joshua, Judges, Samuel, and Kings, considered by many to have formed originally one whole (B), were written under Josiah (see p. 79) and revised during the Exile. Chronicles, together with Ezra and Nehemiah (C), was written by a Levite in the fourth century B.C. Just as with (A), the authors of (B) and (C) employed all kinds of traditional material of differing type and origin; they too were strongly guided in the compilation of their books by the spiritual needs of their contemporaries and by their vision of the past. From this it follows that the more or less literal retelling of the content of (A), (B), and (C) may not be presented without further comment as 'history'. This word is nowadays reserved for a summing-up of past events based upon a critical investigation of the sources. Anyone compiling a history of Israel must first investigate every statement in the three works to decide in which environment it originated, how much it has altered in the course of being handed down, and why the ultimate adaptor incorporated it into his book in just this form and in this place. These questions must definitely be asked, for many continue to cling unconsciously to the idea of the Biblical historian who, sitting concealed with his legs crossed and a scroll in his lap, notes down without error all that he sees and hears. Critical examination of the texts – corroborated but not supplanted by archaeological discoveries – is necessary despite suggestions in certain popular books. Such examination often leads to hypotheses where one would prefer certainties, especially so far as period I of our plan is concerned. Here hypothesis must be preferred to false certainty, out of respect for the Bible.

But are not the *Qumrân* texts of any help? No, the sect established here (for more detail, see pp. 145f.) already knew the three records as canonised holy scripture. In the sacred atmosphere of their writing room, seated at long tables (→facing, top), they carefully copied the holy books, dipping their fingers into the water-filled cavities whenever they wrote the most holy name of God (→ facing, foot). Their Biblical scrolls (→ 60★) are extremely important for the study of the Biblical books which had achieved a definitive form long before their time; but they do not tell us how these books came to be recorded.

THE PATRIARCHS

As no other nation of antiquity Israel preserved and cherished the memories of its origin. In the time of the Judges the tribes were already accustomed, during the offering of the first fruits in Yahweh's sanctuary, to profess their origin in these words: 'A wandering Aramaean was my father; and he went down into Egypt . . . and there he became a nation, great, mighty, and populous. And the Egyptian treated us harshly, and afflicted us and laid upon us hard bondage. Then we cried to the Lord the God of our fathers, and the Lord heard our voice . . . and the Lord brought us out of Egypt with a mighty hand . . . and He brought us unto this place and gave us this land, . . . and behold, now I bring the first of the fruit of the ground which Thou, O Lord, hast given me'. From the use of the personal pronoun one sees how strongly the Israelite felt himself one with his forefathers. It is also clear that even this early profession of faith (handed down in Dt 26 : 5-10) already contains the elements of the great themes which dominate the Pentateuch: the wandering fathers of the tribes who founded a nation in Egypt; the slavery and deliverance; the leading of the people to the Promised Land (only the theme of Mount Sinai and the Covenant is missing here). The first theme is developed in the familiar stories of Genesis 12-50 concerning the adventures of Abraham and Sarah, their son Isaac, and the latter's twin sons Esau and Jacob, of whom the last named, after Joseph's marvellous career, settles in Egypt with all his family.

These stories, which are linked together by the recurring theme of God's promises and His personal guidance of the main characters, appear, on analysis, to be an extraordinary amalgamation of differing elements of various dates, ranging from popular elements to stories with a profound theological import. According to the Hebrew conception the patriarch lived on in his tribe in a very real sense. For this reason, writers liked to explain a characteristic or experience of the tribe by telling a story about the patriarch, often laying particular stress on the meaning of his name. For instance, at one time, the 'sons of Jacob' formed a tribal unity; and (in the time of David) they conquered the Edomites, who lived in the mountain country of Seir. These facts were amalgamated as follows: the word *edom* means 'red', and *seir* has something to do with 'hairy'. The name Jacob, originally perhaps 'may he (God) protect', was associated by the Israelites with the word *akeb*, 'heel'; a verb, probably derived from this word, has in the third person the form *jacob*, 'he lays snares for the heel, he is artful, he deceives'. The story of the twins, of whom the elder Esau (the ancestor of the Edomites) is 'red' and 'hairy' and whom Jacob seizes by the heel, afterwards to 'deceive' and dominate him (Gn 25 : 22-26) is thus really a piece of folk etymology. The historical event in David's reign is here combined with a much older tradition, that the Edomites were of the same ethnic group as the Israelites, that they were 'twin brothers'. In the same way Israel was conscious of kinship with the trans-

Jordan peoples of Moab and Ammon (whom they nevertheless hated). Their names resembled the Hebrew words for 'father' and 'fatherly', hence the not very edifying story of their common origin from Lot, a nephew of Abraham (Gn 19 : 30–38).

During the Assyrian crisis, the great Isaiah was to characterise the attitude of God's people as faith; later, during and after the Exile, the already centuries-old practice of circumcision obtained its full significance as a symbol of the Covenant. For this reason the attitude of Abraham, prototype of the nation which he bore 'in his loins' is described as faith (Gn 15 : 6) and circumcision obtained an essential place in the covenant of God with him (Gn 17).

These are but a few examples, sufficient, it is hoped, to make it clear that the varied whole of Genesis 12–50 should not be considered merely as the simple account of the experiences of a few individuals who lived in antiquity. These chapters are much richer in meaning. Israel's peculiar historical consciousness was closely bound up with its conviction that it was still the object of God's personal interest, an interest which he had begun to show to the patriarchs. It is precisely for this reason that the memory of the patriarchs remained alive, changing and developing through the ages so that it is now impossible to disentangle those details which most interest us today: what the tribal fathers were like as individuals, what their family relationship was to each other, and what exactly happened to each of them. We are obliged to be content with a few main lines which, however, fit extremely well into the picture we now possess of the situation in the east towards the middle of the second millennium B.C.

Originating from Ur, Abraham's family settled near Haran (→ 61★). The names of several cities in that region appear in the genealogy of Abraham (cf. Haran, Nahor, Til-taruhi, Sarugi, and Phaliga, and Haran and Nahor, 'brothers' of Abraham, and Terah, Serug, and Peleg, his 'ancestors' (Gn 11 : 18–26). A group of the clan, Abraham and Lot, the 'father' of Moab and Ammon, journeyed southwards from here to Canaan, without, however, abandoning all contact with those who had remained behind in Aram-naharaim, or Paddan-aram as the region around Haran was also called. They lived as pastoral nomads and travelled with their sheep, goats, and donkeys from one watering-place to another (→ 66, top). They liked to pitch their tents (cf. facing, top), in the country between the waterless plains and the densely populated regions of the towns. One of their routes lay through the valley of the Jabbok (→ facing, foot, note the two tents) where Penuel (also spelled Peniel) lay, into the valley of the Jordan, past Succoth, now a striking tell (→ 67, top), across the river to the plain in front of Shechem, in the heart of the country (→ 67, foot, 68–69, described on p. 25). Across the central mountain ridge they travelled southwards, past Bethel and Hebron where age-old traditions concerning the origin of the Dead Sea and the remarkable rock formations (→ 70★) were linked with their passage (Gn 18, 19), to wander finally in the Negeb, the land of the south, and from there, driven by hunger, to descend towards the fertile Delta. Around 1890 B.C. the Egyptian ruler Chnumhotep had a group of such Semitic nomads depicted on a wall of his tomb (→ 62★). With their multi-coloured garments, their arms, their waterskins and musical instruments, they give a good picture of what Israel's forefathers must have been like.

EXODUS FROM THE HOUSE OF BONDAGE

Of the countless early texts found in Egypt, not one makes any reference to the sojourn of the sons of Jacob in the Delta. One finds no mention of Moses nor of the miraculous escape of the Hebrews across the Red Sea. At the same time, in the Bible narratives, in the books of the patriarchs and in Exodus, the names of the Pharaohs concerned are passed over in silence. This raises the question of where the Bible stories must be located within the framework of the now familiar non-Biblical history.

Roughly along the line now followed by the Suez canal, the Pharaohs of the 19th century B.C. built a chain of forts to protect their land against the multitudes of famished nomads from Canaan who were attracted by the fertility of the Delta. They were, however, allowed to enter as traders, as we saw on the painting of chief Ibsha and his family (→ 62*). The former bears above his name a title which means 'ruler of a foreign land'. When, ca 1700 B.C. the chain of fortresses proved too weak to repel an invasion of mixed racial groups from Canaan and beyond, who ruled lower Egypt for more than a century, they too were given the same title: *ḥq'ḫ's.t*, which became in Greek 'Hyksos'. Many scholars believe that the settlement of Jacob's sons in Egypt must be sought in this historical background. Joseph's career would be comprehensible in the court of a Pharaoh who himself originated from Canaan. Around 1570 B.C. the Hyksos were expelled from Thebes in the south, and thus began the great epoch during which the Pharaohs from Amenophis I to Thothmes III expanded their territory northwards as far as the Euphrates. This kingdom collapsed under the rule of the unworldly, religious reformer Amenophis IV who called himself Akhenaton (see p. 44). Horemheb was the name of the general who attempted to put down the revolt which had flared up in Palestine under Akhenaton's weak son-in-law Tutankhamon, and ended by becoming Pharaoh himself (1345–1318). The magnificent reliefs from his tomb near Memphis have found their way to various museums – some of the finest are housed in the Rijksmuseum voor Oudheden in Leiden. Detail, facing: Egyptian officers lead two Palestinian captives in the triumphal procession of Horemheb. Another panel shows a group of Syrians who, as the accompanying text explains, 'not knowing how to remain alive', beg admittance to Egypt, 'according to the custom of your fathers from time immemorial'. After Horemheb the restoration was continued and attained a last peak of power and prosperity under Rameses II (1301–1234).

During the first years of his reign Rameses waged a series of bitter wars against the Hittites who were pressing in from Asia Minor. He concluded a famous peace treaty in 1280. The Egyptian version can still be read on temple walls in Thebes and the Hittite has been found in Babylonian cuneiform writing upon clay tablets. It is generally thought that the Exodus of the Hebrews under Moses must have taken place during the reign of this Pharaoh. This theory is supported by a number of Palestinian archaeological data, such as traces of destruction and migration of inhabitants which must have occurred in various places at roughly the same time, *ca* 1200 B.C. In addition, the situation in Egypt seems an ideal background for the Biblical data. After the expulsion of the Hyksos rulers, many 'Asiatics' had remained behind in the Delta. They were disliked and mistrusted, and it is understandable that Rameses should have chosen his building labourers from among their ranks. On the well known scene from the tomb of Rekhmire in Thebes, painted *ca* 1460, one sees a typical 'Asiatic' among the brick-bakers (→ facing). Under Rameses they undoubtedly formed the majority of those who had to perform this wearying task. These people who, with other prisoners of war and slaves, formed a distinct social class, were called the *'apiru*. Some scholars connect this term with the word *'ibri*, Hebrew, which is indeed employed in the stories of Joseph and the Exodus with striking consistency.

During the increasingly heavy forced labour of his group in the land of Goshen Moses had had his mysterious encounter with God in the majestic surroundings of Mount Sinai, in which he experienced the greatness and solicitude of the 'God of the fathers'. Through narrow passes, through spectacularly coloured rocks (→ 76, top), one penetrates into the granite heart of the peninsula to emerge suddenly on to a plateau with a towering range in the background; the left-hand peak, slightly to the rear, is the mountain which centuries of tradition have designated as the mountain of Moses (→ 76, foot). The caravan in this photograph is en route for a point in the shadowed valley to the left, where the famous monastery of St Catherine lies. It can be seen on the following plate (→ 77*), taken from the opposite direction, so that the plateau lies in the background. Did Moses lead his group of Hebrews, that 'mixed multitude', which included a considerable 'rabble' (Ex 12 : 38, Num 11 : 4) straight to these majestic surroundings after a miraculous crossing of an arm of the Red Sea? Or must we agree with the scholars who hold that the Exodus took place along the northern route? The miraculous crossing would then have taken place on the coast, east of Pelusium (see map on p. 129), where a mountain of God had also been known from ancient times. The localisations in the Biblical story give no definite confirmation one way or the other (Sea of Reeds, Pi-hahiroth, Migdol, Baal-zephon...). Only the provisional finishing point of the journey is certain, the region of springs around Kadesh in south Palestine (it can just be seen on Map 2, facing p. 84). Moses and his work have sometimes been compared to a mountain that rises up out of the mist. The outline can be seen only vaguely, but we know that it is there, majestic and imposing.

The Exodus and the Covenant form the basis of Israel's further history. The faith of Israel preserved the nucleus of the facts and extended and enhanced them in daily life, not least in the ever-repeated religious ceremonies. The memory of the exact circumstances grew dim. The historian is compelled to grope in the dark. He is not nearly so certain of the course of events during the Exodus as the film makers of Hollywood, yet much more than they he is conscious of the far-reaching historical effects of this event upon the faith and history of Israel.

SETTLEMENT IN CANAAN

After remaining for many years in the land of Kadesh, in the extreme south of Palestine, Moses went northeastwards with his Hebrews to the 'plains of Moab" across the Jordan facing Jericho. It is no longer possible to form a complete whole from the scraps of tradition concerning the route followed which are set down in the books of Numbers and Deuteronomy. Moses undoubtedly crossed the deep cleft in the Transjordan highland called in our Bible 'the brook Arnon' (→ facing, top). Biblical tradition localises his leave-taking and death on the top of Mount Nebo (→ facing, foot, viewed from the south). From the top of this mountain, on which lie the ruins of a church and monastery dating from the sixth century, looking across the Jordan valley, 3,500 ft. below (right on this photograph), one can indeed survey the whole of the hilly central region of Palestine from Hebron to Galilee including Mount Carmel. Southwards the eye covers a large section of the Dead Sea, and towards the north, in clear weather, one can see as far as the Sea of Galilee and snow-covered Mount Hermon, 112 miles from Mount Nebo. The land which throughout all these years Moses had seen in his mind's eye as the ultimate goal of his life's work lay here stretched out before him. But the joy of leading his people into the Promised Land was denied him. This task was reserved for Joshua.

The plan of the Biblical book that bears his name is strikingly simple and its geography (at least so far as the campaigns are concerned) is easy to show on a map (see Map 3, facing p. 85). In accordance with the divine command (Ch. 1) Joshua sent men to spy out the land on the other side of the Jordan (Ch. 2), crossed the Jordan (whose waters divided as did those of the Red Sea) with the twelve tribes (Chs. 3, 4), had the people circumcised and celebrated the Passover (Ch. 5), and then conquered Jericho (Ch. 6). After this, following a natural curve (→ 82, top) he crossed the central mountainous country and took Ai (Chs. 7, 8). He spared Gibeon (→ 82, centre, see 81) and its allied cities (Ch. 9) after which he defeated a number of rulers, among them the king of Lachish (→ 82, foot), and conquered the whole of the south (Ch. 10); then, after the battle by the waters of Merom and the destruction of the important royal city of Hazor (→ 83) he took possession of the northern part of Palestine and thus became master of the whole land (Ch. 12). After this the entire country, including the Transjordan which had already been occupied, was divided among the twelve tribes (Chs. 13–22). Joshua then delivered his last exhortations, died, and was buried (Chs. 23, 24).

It is evident that we have here a simplified version of a complicated series of events. This simplification is understandable. The book of Joshua was written under King Josiah (640–609 B.C.), probably as the first section of a larger chronicle (see p. 58) and was revised during the Exile. This work might be considered as a sort of national epic, bearing in mind that in Israel national and religious were one.

For Israel's dwelling in Palestine formed an essential part of the creed (see p. 63). Yahweh was not god in general; Yahweh was He who had promised the land of Canaan to the fathers and, faithful to His word, had led their descendants out of Egypt to make of them His own people who would inhabit His land. One can thus appreciate something of the tremendous crisis when the Assyrians conquered the larger part of Palestine in 721. One also senses, however, the revival of national and religious aspirations following the rapid decline of Assyria in the years after 650. Soon Israel would once again inhabit undisturbed the entire land of Yahweh. At this period all the earlier traditions still living were assembled in a sort of epic, not solely out of love for the past but also as an expression of revived faith, as well as a stimulus and guiding principle for the national restoration. This is why we are given at the outset a simple and eloquent picture of Israel's entry into the Promised Land. Aided by Yahweh's mighty arm, Joshua entered this land at the head of the twelve tribes. He conquered the entire land, and each tribe was allotted its portion. 'Not one of all the good promises which the Lord had made to the house of Israel had failed; all came to pass (Jos 21 : 45). But just as all the good things which the Lord your God promised concerning you have been fulfilled for you, so the Lord will bring upon you all the evil things, until he have destroyed you from off this good land which the Lord your God has given you (Jos 23 : 15)'.

Within this impressive framework the composers of the epic brought together all kinds of traditional material of ancient and more recent date, giving little thought to the question of whether or not it all fitted in with the historical background. It is, for example, now almost certain that a number of the cities allotted to Judah in Joshua 15 did not yet exist in Joshua's day: in order to fill out the bare statement 'Judah obtained this particular region' the compilers used an administrative list dating from the time of Judah's kings. They also used older sources from which it appears that some tribes had great difficulty in taking possession of Canaanite cities (see Jos 17 : 11–13; cf. Jg 1 : 27–35). It apparently did not worry them that these details were in direct contradiction to their idea that Joshua personally conquered all the cities. We can see that the Bible text itself brings up the question of how exactly the settlement in Canaan took place. The theories proposed by scholars are still widely divergent. From the fact that no mention is made of a campaign in central Palestine and from the certainly ancient fact of the renewal of the tribal alliance at Shechem, the heart of this region (Jos 24), they conclude that the newcomers found related tribes there. Had these arrived from Egypt before them or had they never been there at all? In both cases then the idea of the twelve tribes entering together through the Jordan near Jericho must be the result of simplification. The same is true of many chapters in the Pentateuch dealing with the journey through the desert. Moreover, there are indications that the tribe of Judah contained groups which had penetrated into Canaan from the south. This confirms the impression that the entry of the tribes was in reality a very complex event. In the following chapter we shall see that archaeology has made the problem more complicated rather than solved it, which warns us to be cautious about putting too much faith in the theory that the excavations bear out the facts of the Bible.

Sultantepe

Tarsus

Carchemish

Haran

Pethor
home of
Baalam

ARAM-NAHARAIM
'Aram of the two rivers'

Home of Abraham's family
Rebekah came from here Jacob
stayed here for a long time with
Laban

AMANUS

Alalakh

Aleppo

Euphrates

Balikh

Qarqar

 Râs Shamra
Ugarit

Orontes

Hamath

Arvad

Zemar

Qatna

Arqa   Sin

Kadesh

DITERRANEAN

SEA

Gebal
Byblos

Lebo-hamath

Ba'albek

Sidon

Damascus

S Y R O -
A R A B I A N
D E S E R T

Zarephath

Tyre

Dan

Hazor

Acco

Ashtaroth

Dor

Megiddo

Edrei

Taanach

Beth-shan

Ham

Salecah

Dothan

Pella

Busra

Tirzah

Succoth

Jabbok

Shechem

Penuel

Mahanaim

Joppa

Mizpah

Gezer   Jericho

Jerusalem

Bethlehem

Gaza

Hebron

Gerar

Plain of
Kirinthaim

Sharuhen

Beer-sheba

Zoar

EGEB

Rehoboth

Hazazon-tamar

In the shallowest part of the
Dead Sea are usually
located Valley of Siddim,
Sodom, Gomorrah, Admah,
Zeboim

f drought and
e nomads
to the fertile

Bozrah

Punon

LEBANON

ANTI-LEBANON

HERMON

CANAAN

Region of the Jordan

SALT SEA

2

0   10   20   30   40   50 miles

THE WANDERINGS
OF THE
PATRIARCHS

On the map are indicated:

1. The places named in the stories of Genesis 12-50

2. A few Biblical localities lying
    outside Palestine proper

3. Only a few of the many cities
    which flourished here during the
    second millennium B.C.

East of this line the average
annual rainfall is less than 4 inches

PALESTINE

Geographical survey showing the most important excavations

- - - Courses of principal highways (generalised)

Dan

UPPER GALILEE

Lake Huleh 6ft

Hazor III

Capernaum

LOWER GALILEE

SEA OF GALILEE -700ft

BASHAN

Acco

(HAIFA)

T. Abu Hawâm II

CARMEL

Nazareth

TABOR

Yarmuk

PLAIN OF JEZREEL

Megiddo I, II

Caesarea III

Taanach I

GILBOA

Beth-shan II

Dothan III

PLAIN OF SHARON

Samaria I, II

Tirzah III

Penu

Shechem II, III

GREAT

SEA

EPHRAIM

Jordan

GILEAD

T. el-Qasîleh III

Shiloh II

Jaffa

Baal-hazor

Mizpah II

Geba

Jericho I, II, III

Gezer I, II

Gibeon III

Ekron

Jerusalem

Teleilât el-Ghassûl II

Ashdod

Bethlehem

Kh. Qumrân III

Ashkelon

JUDAH

HILL COUNTRY

Dibo

WILDERNESS

Lachish II

T. el-Hesy I

Hebron

Gaza

DEAD

PHILISTIA

T. Beit Mirsim II

SEA

-1290ft

Tel-'Ajjûl II

LOWLAND

Arnon

T. Jemmeh II

MOAB

Tel-Fâr'ah II

Beer-sheba III

0   5   10   15   20 miles

FROM JOSHUA TO SAUL

According to some archaeologists, the Biblical account of a wholesale destructive invasion of the Israelites in Canaan is confirmed by traces of the simultaneous destruction of Bethel, Lachish, and *Tell Beit Mirsim* (probably Debir), occurring some time before 1200 B.C. This conviction is in some measure supported by the testimony of the Israelite archaeologists who have been working on a large scale and very ably since 1955 at Hazor in the north (→ 83*). On the other side of the scale, however, must be accounted the negative results obtained in Jericho and Ai. The lower layers of Jericho, which have been investigated in annual campaigns since 1952 by Miss Kenyon, appear to contain settlements from the 8th millennium B.C., which means that Jericho is the oldest known city in the world. No certain trace, however, has yet been found of a Jericho dating from the 13th century B.C. or thereabouts. The town of Ai, whose conquest is described in Joshua 8, has long been localised in the immense ruin hill a mile and a half southeast of Bethel. It is known to the inhabitants as *et-Tell*, 'the tell', which agrees with the Hebrew name meaning 'heap of rubble'. This tell was excavated in the years 1933–4 and it was found that the site was already inhabited *ca* 3300 B.C., was completely destroyed *ca* 2400 B.C. and remained a heap of ruins until *ca* 1000 B.C. when the Israelites settled there. In Joshua's time Ai was thus what its name implies, a heap of ruins. How is this to be reconciled with the Bible? We give here four solutions proposed: *a*) the story in Joshua 8 originated much later in order to explain the presence of the immense heap of rubble; *b*) it possesses a core of historical truth, for the inhabitants of nearby Bethel had entrenched themselves in Ai against the invading Israelites; *c*) the story originally concerned the conquest of Bethel, but when this town later became a flourishing Israelite city, Ai was made the subject of the narrative; and finally *d*) Ai must be localised, not in *et-Tell*, but elsewhere. It is in any case clear that for the precise circumstances of Israel's settlement in Canaan one must fall back on conjecture. It is perhaps best to hold a middle view between a 'blitzkrieg' under Joshua, followed by total occupation, and a lengthy peaceful penetration.

Certainly the next two centuries lived on in the memory of Israel as the heroic period. The hero Joshua, whose original name Hoshea, according to Numbers 13 : 16, was changed by Moses to an explicitly 'Yahwistic' form, 'Yahweh is salvation', or 'grant salvation' (pronounced 'Jesus' by the Alexandrian Jews) was followed by a number of heroic popular leaders who indeed brought 'salvation', that is victory over the enemy, release from oppression, peace, and prosperity. The compilers of the national epic under King Josiah (see p. 79) gathered together a number of traditions concerning these figures in the present book of Judges. They thought best to serve their contemporaries, who had suffered the oppression of the Assyrians, by constantly emphasising in this narrative series the underlying causes: it was Yahweh, their God who, on account of the defection of the Israelites, was compelled to deliver them up to the oppressor. When in their need, they turned to Him again, He sent them a bringer of salvation, a 'redeemer' in the person of a judge. Notwithstanding their desire to transmit the lessons of history (cf. the prologue, Jg 2 : 6–3 : 4 and for example 10 : 6–16) the compilers respected the original material. Thus the modern historian can find in their works reliable information concerning the life of the tribes during these centuries. They formed a sort of sacral confederation, probably of the type also found in Greece: living about a sanctuary recognised by all, each tribe had in turn to attend to the sacrificial cult for a month. This seems to be the origin of the division into twelve tribes, in Israel and also among some neighbouring peoples (cf. the 12 'sons' of Nahor and of Ishmael, Gn 22 : 20–24 and 25 : 13–16). After Gilgal, Shiloh, where the Ark of the Covenant was kept, functioned as the central sanctuary and also as a place of pilgrimage.

The principal campaigns of the Judges against foreign oppressors are broadly indicated on Map 3, facing p. 85. In the north we find that of Deborah and Barak against Canaanite city rulers, where the mighty Mount Tabor (→ 84★) served as a rallying point. The poetical account of this struggle (Jg 5), probably composed while the events were fresh in the memory (*ca* 1125 B.C.) and transmitted almost unchanged, tells us a great deal about the common faith and inter-tribal relations. Also indicated are Gideon's action against camel-riding nomads from the east who made destructive raids into Israelite territory, Jephthah's action against the Ammonites, and Ehud's struggle against Moabite oppressors.

The greatest obstacle to the further development of the tribes of Israel was the Philistines. This people, who had taken part in the great migration which around 1200 B.C. had caused a great upheaval in all the eastern parts of the Mediterranean and whom Rameses III (1197–1165) had with difficulty prevented from entering Egypt, had settled on the southern coastal plain. After a few decades of continual skirmishing with the nearest Israelites (this was the background which gave rise to popular tales like those concerning Samson and his famous exploits) these uncircumcised non-Semites began to penetrate farther into the central mountainous country. Superior in their knowledge of the use of iron which they had brought with them from their land of origin (Kaftor, said the Israelites, i.e. perhaps the cultural centre, Crete), they truly terrorised the Israelites. The gripping narrative series which the compilers of the great chronicle (see p. 79) assembled in the first book of Samuel clearly shows how critical the situation was when the Ark of the Covenant, symbol of the unity of the tribes, was captured by the Philistines and when the latter occupied a large area of Israelite territory. Even the common pilgrimage centre of Shiloh was then destroyed. In reading the first book of Samuel the imagination may be supplemented by the certainly accurate portrait of a Philistine and a Semitic inhabitant of Canaan (→ facing★) and also by a photograph of the pass between Michmash and Geba, the scene of Jonathan's heroic deed (→ 88★). Finally, to illustrate the last chapter of 1 Samuel, there is the view of the mountains of Gilboa (→ 89, foot★). Here Israel was crushingly defeated and Saul, her first king, slain.

JERUSALEM - CITY OF DAVID
AND OF GOD

After the tragic death of King Saul upon the mountains of Gilboa David, until that time a vassal of the Philistines at Ziklag and at the same time the firm defender of the Judaean farmers in the frontier regions, was in Hebron proclaimed king of the tribe of Judah and anointed. He thereby reaped the reward of a shrewd and patient policy which he continued to pursue throughout the coming years in his dealings with the rest of Saul's kingdom. Finally, envoys from the northern tribes came to Hebron to ask if he would be their king. When David consented and was anointed king of all Israel *ca* 1000 B.C. he inaugurated a new era in the history of Yahweh's people.

It was David who transformed the sacral tribal alliance into an important kingdom, thereby enriching Israel's religious life with new perspectives and new forms of expression. For at that time a nation's king was considered a sacral figure, a representative on earth of the national god, very closely linked with him and often even called a 'son' of the god. This conception was strong in Egypt and David's kingship appears to have been especially influenced from this direction. According to an old tradition which is again finding credence among an increasing number of modern scholars, it was David himself to whom one of the court poets addressed the words of Psalm 110: 'The Lord says to my lord: "Sit at my right hand till I make your enemies your footstool." ' In another text the king himself says that Yahweh spoke to him: 'You are my son, today I have begotten you' (Ps 2 : 7). To address such words to a man, a farmer's son from Bethlehem, was unheard of in Israel, but in Egypt it was customary. For an illustration of the second text compare the obelisk of Hatshepsut (see p. 44). Both sections of the verse taken from Psalm 110 are illustrated by a picture of Thothmes III seated at the right hand of the god Amon, and a throne of Tutankhamon of which the footstool shows the nine traditional enemies of Egypt (→ facing★).

These few examples taken from the abundant material raise the question of how such Egyptian influences penetrated the office and undoubtedly also the ceremonial of the young royal court. The historical information which the Bible has preserved concerning David and his work is plentiful and valuable but yet not sufficient to provide a definite answer to a modern historical query. The wealth of information must be attributed to the fact that David himself was an extraordinarily fascinating person. Even during his lifetime stories grew up around him, mostly about his youth and his activities under Saul. A number of these stories are incorporated in the books of Samuel although the compiler did not trouble overmuch about the logical connection of the recorded events.

In his later years too the figure of David remained so enthralling that a learned and wise man from his entourage was inspired to write a sort of biography. The strong and sober style of this genuine masterpiece and above all the feeling for the human element, incorporated almost unchanged in the national chronicle (2 S 9–20 and 1 K 1,2), render it far superior to any other biographical work of that period or of long afterwards. The author wrote this work during Solomon's reign. His main theme was obviously the establishment of David's dynasty; how, after many complications and setbacks, the great ruler finally obtained his successor in Solomon. That this question was of immense national and thus religious importance is obvious to anyone who carefully studies the promises made by the God of Israel to David and his house, transmitted to him by the prophet Nathan and, judging from various psalms, regularly commemorated in the religious ceremonial (2 S 7, cf. Ps 89, 132, etc.). One result of this limited aim is that this magnificent story tells us as little as the more popular traditions about what we should really like to know: how David extended and consolidated his power, how he administered and regulated the economy of his kingdom, what foreign influences there were at court, etc. The modern historian can only give an incomplete answer to these queries, gleaned from scattered notes (e.g. concerning David's conquests in 2 S 8) and casual remarks in the Biblical books themselves, from non-Biblical material (objects, pictures, and texts), and many hypotheses.

One important measure should be singled out in this short survey. When he accepted the kingship of the northern tribes, one enclave remained between their region and the land of Judah, the city of Jerusalem with its surrounding territory. The Philistines, alarmed by the sudden increase in power of their former vassal, gathered there with a great army in order to overpower him on his first journey to the north. David defeated them near Baal-perazim, slightly northwest of Jerusalem, and so decisively that they never again constituted a serious threat to Israel. Three centuries later Isaiah commemorated this victory as a mighty work of God (Is 28 : 21). David then abolished the enclave. The small but strong citadel of Jerusalem lay upon a mountain ridge, both sides of which were extremely steep. At the foot the spring Gihon had its source. In case of siege the inhabitants could cut off the access to this spring from the valley and reach the water from within the city by means of a tunnel hewn out of the rock (see the sketch → 107, foot*), a system that was also applied in other towns of Canaan, in Megiddo, Gezer, and Gibeon (→ 106, top, and foot, left*), and which was later perfected in Jerusalem by King Hezekiah (→ 106, foot, right*).

Thanks to a daring exploit by Joab who, if we read the text aright, crept up through the water tunnel – in Jerusalem part of it was a vertical well! – and surprised the defenders (2 S 5 : 8; 1 Ch 11 : 6), David conquered the citadel. He at once made Jerusalem, of old also called Zion, the capital of his kingdom. Formerly a dividing wall between Judah and the other tribes, this city, captured by David himself and thus called by his name (see 2 S 12 : 28), was to become the central point of the new state of the twelve tribes. For this reason David quickly transferred there the Ark of the Covenant which throughout the preceding troubled years had remained half forgotten in Kiriath-jearim. Thus did the 'city of David' take over the rôle of ancient Shiloh which for fully a century and a half had been the centre of the tribal federation.

From the point of view of world history the importance of these first acts of David's reign can scarcely be over-estimated. One has only to consider the full import of the ideas which became linked for good at that moment of history: the God of Israel came to dwell in the city of 'his Anointed' as David's title was, *Messiah* in Hebrew, *Christos* in Greek. Ruling from God's capital this Christos had the task of ruling justly and, by settling all disputes, of causing righteousness to reign first in his own kingdom and then beyond. The promises transmitted by Nathan also concerned the coming rulers from the house of David and in fact contained the seeds of Israel's hope for a 'messianic' realm of peace for the whole of mankind, an expectation expressed in so many psalms and prophecies. The centre of these prophecies is always Zion, the city of David and of God.

Under the glorious reign of David's son Solomon (*ca* 970–930 B.C.) Jerusalem was magnificently expanded to the north. There, higher than the city itself and more exposed to the wind, to make the winnowing easier (→ 121, foot), lay the threshing floor of Araunah (Ornan) which David had bought from this Jebusite in order to erect an altar there and to offer sacrifice. Upon this spot, with the help of architects, artists, and material from Phoenicia (including cedars from Lebanon), Solomon built a temple for Yahweh in which he placed the Ark of the Covenant. He undoubtedly enlarged the surface around the threshing floor by building an artificial terrace. We shall never know the exact dimensions of this terrace nor the exact site of the imposing palace that Solomon built between the temple and city. For Herod had the terrace enlarged into an enormous temple square. This is now the site of the Mosque of Omar, and as the deeply venerated rock is the second holy place of Islam after Mecca it has never been possible to excavate the site.

Looking northwards through the Kidron valley one can see the elevation of the terrace, the site of Solomon's palace and temple (→ 96, top). It also dominates the three aerial photos of Jerusalem which are grouped together so that, together with the folding Map 4 (facing p. 85) they may offer a good general view of the ground relief, the historical development of the city, and the position of the principal holy places. Fortunately the description of Solomon's temple and its furniture (1 K 6–7), which is hard to understand, can now be illustrated by various archaeological discoveries. On the clear ground plan, to which a remarkable parallel was found at Hazor (→ 103*), fairly reliable reconstructions can be made (→ 102, top*), while the descriptions of objects for the religious ceremonies, e.g. laver and altar, can also be made clear with concrete examples (→ 98, foot*). The same holds good for the ornamentations (→ 101*). Excavators have found remains of Solomon's constructions outside Jerusalem, at Megiddo among other places, where the city gate (see the reconstructed sketch which shows the gate with its fortifications and buildings, → 102, foot) has now an exact parallel at Hazor (→ 83, foot, left foreground).

Although he lost some of the regions conquered by his father, Solomon increased his wealth by large-scale world trade. His merchant fleet, built and manned by Phoenicians, sailed from the harbour near Ezion-geber on the Gulf of Elath and made journeys to the distant gold country of Ophir. The excavations at Ezion geber even provided a supplement to the awe-inspired account in the Bible in which Solomon's glory already seems to have become legendary: the remains of a large metal industry were found there. Within a few decades, therefore, the farming people of Israel were called upon to assimilate a succession of innovations. Many of these were of foreign, mainly Egyptian, origin.

Jerusalem was an extremely old city, dependent for centuries upon the Pharaohs (like, for example Beth-Shan, → 53, foot*), and possessing venerable religious traditions. The Bible itself records that of Melchizedek, king and priest of God Most High (Gn 14 : 18–24). We are not told that David killed the Jebusites and their king; on the contrary, his respect for the possession of Araunah is striking. It is possible that David, later considered as the great organiser of the temple service, adopted elements from these traditions, including some which concerned his own rôle as king of Yahweh's people. Certainly Egyptians and officials trained in Egypt assisted in the organisation of the new kingdom. Solomon married a daughter of the Pharaoh. This being so it appears possible to form an idea of many of the activities of Solomon's court, music and dance for example, with the help of Egyptian reliefs (→ facing, top).

All these innovations were bound to arouse fierce reactions among a people so attached to its traditions. Especially unpopular was the new administrative division of the kingdom into twelve districts, which Solomon introduced (see 1 K 4 : 7–20 and Map 5) and which deliberately severed the old tribal connections. On the other hand the political reorganisation had its advantages.

Solomon was possessed of superhuman wisdom (1 K 4 : 29–34) and the legends about it were manifold. By 'wisdom' one must understand not only an encyclopedic and ordered knowledge of everything under the sun, but also the concise definition of all forms of human behaviour, in particular the art of being the perfect gentleman. This art, so indispensable for the attainment of a successful career, had been practised for centuries in Egypt.

The nucleus of the earliest collections of proverbs in the Bible (Pr 10–22 and 25–29) probably originated in the circles of the royal officials. These proverbs contain no mention of Israel, alliance, election, holiness or the like, but during Solomon's reign or the following century a work was composed in which the deepest religious convictions of Israel were set down in an imposing manner. In a style which equals that of the already mentioned court chronicle of David but which is much more pronouncedly religious, an author (or a group of authors) laid the foundations of the so-called Yahwistic chronicle. In an attempt perhaps to preserve the old traditions of the disintegrating confederation, a coherent narrative was made of Israel's past, from Abraham to the death of Moses. It was preceded by a profound introduction which began with the general human aspect, the creation of *adam*, that is, of man, in paradise. The stories of the fall, the fratricide, the flood and the tower of Babel represented the rapid growth of evil with as a result the total disintegration of a humanity which Yahweh had intended to form a happy community. Against this background was projected the call of Abraham, that is, of Israel: through him Yahweh wished to make mankind one again and to heap humanity with blessings.

98

JUDAH AND ISRAEL

Immediately after Solomon's death, *ca* 930 B.C., the inner cleavage of the Kingdom, already obvious at times under David, and aggravated by Solomon's manner of ruling, expressed itself by a split. Then the old cry was heard again in the North: 'What portion have we in David? We have no inheritance in the son of Jesse. To your tents, O Israel!' (1 K 12 : 16, cf. 2 S 20 : 1). The rebels, assembled in the ancient meeting-place of Shechem, chose as king a certain Jeroboam. A born leader, this man of the tribe of Ephraim had been appointed by Solomon as chief inspector of the forced labour carried out by 'the house of Joseph', which included not only Ephraim and Manasseh but all the northern tribes. On account of his revolutionary tendencies he had been obliged to hide in Egypt from the king's police. According to I Kings chapter 11 these tendencies had been strengthened in him by Ahijah, a prophet from Shiloh, the old religious centre of the tribal alliance, also in Ephraim. Designated by a prophet and proclaimed by the people, just as Saul and David had been, Jeroboam began to rule as king in Shechem.

The Disruption was never to be healed, and from now on the northerners, with Jeroboam as their king, can be called Israel, as distinct from Judah over which Solomon's son Rehoboam ruled as king.

The political division was of course accompanied by a religious one. Jeroboam appointed two sanctuaries in his kingdom for the worship of Yahweh, one of them in the north, in Dan, the other in Bethel, $9\frac{1}{2}$ miles north of Jerusalem. Its foundation was attributed to the patriarch Jacob, also called Israel. In both Dan and Bethel the king caused to be set up the statue of a bull-calf, covered in gold. This animal had been from ancient times a popular symbol of the divinity who grants life and fruitfulness. Recently a small statue of a bull was found in a pre-Israelite sanctuary in Hazor (→ facing, top). Jeroboam sought in this way to render the worship of Yahweh more attractive. Perhaps he meant these statues to be the pedestals upon which Yahweh, the giver of all fertility, is invisibly enthroned. In the region around Canaan several pictures have been found representing a divinity standing upon the animal linked with him (→ 53, foot, left*). Sometimes their likeness is replaced by a symbol, for example a heavenly body, placed above the animal. But the common people in Israel would not be able to make this distinction and would begin to worship the calf as Yahweh, just as the pagans served their Baals, with profound effect upon their life and thought.

Two centuries later Isaiah, as attached to Zion, the abode of the Holy One of Israel, as to the house of David, was to consider this Disruption whereby 'Ephraim fell away from Judah' as the greatest calamity that ever befell the people of God (Is 7 : 17). How Yahweh judged Jeroboam's deed appeared abundantly clear to the prophet and his disciples in 721, when Assyria wiped the entire Northern Kingdom from the map. During Sennacherib's campaign against Judah in 701, only

Jerusalem was spared, by a miraculous dispensation. It thus became increasingly clear that the God of Israel wished to be worshipped only in Jerusalem, nowhere else, not even upon the ancient and venerable 'high places' or local sanctuaries in the district around the capital. Although King Hezekiah took all measures to this end it was above all Josiah who carried out the evident wish of Yahweh, unambiguously expressed in the book of Deuteronomy.

The compilers of the books of Kings (the third part of the great chronicle, see p. 58) were guided by the same conviction. They derived their basic information about the history of the two kingdoms from the official royal annals or from extracts. These gave them the dates of the outline within which they dealt with every reign: 'In the ... th year of X, king of Judah (Israel), Y became king of Israel (Judah) and ruled for ... years'. Then follows their judgment. All the kings of Israel were reproved because they continued in the path of Jeroboam who had led Israel into sin. In other words, because they did not put an end to the division of the kingdom. This is the reason for the lesson in narrative form – rather complicated for modern readers – in 1 Kings 13 (see also 14) and the summary of 2 Kings 17. The kings of Judah were all of David's dynasty and the house of Yahweh was the royal temple of them all. And yet only eight of them were accounted good, six with the spiteful remark that under them 'the high places were not removed'. Only Hezekiah and Josiah receive unmixed praise. The convictions of the chroniclers also influenced strongly the choice of the material with which they filled in their outline. They held as especially important for contemporaries and descendants stories which had to do with religion, i.e. in which the temple played a rôle or a prophet appeared. We hear about the invasion of Shishak (the first Pharaoh the Bible mentions by name) because Rehoboam paid him a ransom with treasures from the temple. We know a little more about Ahab because he is Elijah's opponent in the fine cycle of stories about this prophet. That Ahab, with 10,000 men and 2,000 war chariots, took part in the battle of Qarqar against Shalmaneser V in 854 B.C. was apparently one of the details which the reader had to look up for himself in the official chronicles, if he was interested. The annals of Judah and Israel no longer exist, but we still have those of the Assyrians, inscribed in clay and stone. It is from this source that we know that Ahab took part in this battle.

From these and other non-Biblical texts and from archaeological data the modern historian can supplement the rather biased material of Kings (and Chronicles, even more biased but with a few valuable additions) thus forming the picture of Israel now found in reliable history books. Thus, in the six lines about Omri, we are told only that he abandoned his capital of Tirzah after six years and built a new one that he called Samaria. What he began to build in Tirzah has been excavated, just beneath the surface of the tell (→ 36★). His palace in Samaria has also been excavated, and the remains of ivory friezes found (→ 101★). We now understand why he changed capitals and esteem him as the greatest ruler of Israel.

In reading the books of Kings the plan on page 116 may prove helpful. The accompanying map indicates the possible sites of most of the places mentioned in the narratives of Samuel, Kings, and Chronicles.

FROM SAUL
TO THE EXILE
The time of the Kings

District of Solomon (1 K 4: 7-19)
Frontiers between Israel, Judah, and the Philistines
Fortress of Rehoboam (2 Ch 11 : 5-10)

Abel-beth-maacah
Dan
Kedesh
VIII
Hazor
GESHUR
IX
Chinnereth
Acco
Aphek
Kabul
CARMEL
Kishon
Gath-hepher
Jokneam
X
En-dor
Shunem
VI
Dor
Megiddo
Jezreel
Beth-arbel
IV
V
Rogelim
Taanach
GILBOA
Ramoth-gilead
Arubboth
Beth-haggan
Beth-shan
Ibleam
Cherith
III
Hepher
Dothan
Jabesh-gilead
Tishbe
Socoh
Bezek
SAMARIA
Thebez
Abel-meholah
Tirzah
Shechem
Pirathon
Succoth
Jabbok
Baal-shalishah
Penuel
Mahanaim
Aphek
Tappuah
VII
Joppa
Zeredah
I
Shiloh
Ramathaim
Gilgal
Jazer
AMMON
Jesanah
Rabbah of the Ammonites
Gimzo
Ephron
Bethel
Beth-horon
XI
Gezer
Mizpah
Jabneel
Aijalon
Gibeon
Geba
Jericho
Gibbethon
Ramah
Gilgal
Mephaath
Ekron
II
Gibeah
Elealeh
Makaz
JERUSALEM
Heshbon
Ashdod
Zorah
XII
Beth-shemesh
Medeba
Libnah
Azekah
Bethlehem
Baal-meon
Ashkelon
Socoh
Etam
Adullam
Netophah
SEA
OF
THE PLAIN
Gath
Moresheth
Tekoa
OR
Mareshah
Beth-zur
Lachish
Ataroth
Hebron
SALT SEA
Dibon
Beth-gamul
Adoraim
Ziph
PHILISTINES
Gaza
Beth-ezel
En-gedi
Aroer
Jattir
Carmel
Arnon
Gerar
Eshtemoa
Maon

MOAB

Beer-sheba

Kir-moab
Kir-hareseth

0   5   10   15   20 miles

5

THE EXPANSION OF ASSYRIA

Limits of expansion of the Assyrian empire

0   100   200   300 miles

*Map labels (top map):*

BLACK SEA

LYCIA

CILICIA

CYPRUS

MEDES

Conquered by Sargon in 717 B.C.;
'Is not Calno like Carchemish?
Is not Hamath like Arpad? Is
not Samaria like Damascus?'
(Is 10:9)

Carchemish
Calno
Haran
Gozan
Khorsabad
Nineveh
Arpad
Battle of Qarqar, 854 B.C.
Qarqar
Hamath
Rezeph
ASSYRIA
Ashur

Byblos

Destroyed in 732 B.C. by
Tiglath-pileser III

Tyre
Damascus
Samaria conquered by Sargon in 721 B.C.
Samaria
AMMON
Jerusalem besieged in vain
by Sennacherib in 701 B.C.
Ashdod
Jerusalem
JUDAH MOAB
Sais
Conquered by Esarhaddon
in 670 B.C.
EDOM
EGYPT
Memphis
Bozra

Babylon
BABYLONIA
Sennacherib destroys Babylon
in 689 B.C.; it is rebuilt by
Esarhaddon
SEA LAND
CHALDAEANS
Ur
ELAM
Susa

Elath

Tema

**THE PERSIAN EMPIRE
AND THE EXPEDITIONS OF
ALEXANDER THE GREAT**

→ Route followed by Alexander the Great

0   200   400   600 miles

*Map labels (bottom map):*

SCYTHIANS

Philippopolis
Pella
MACEDONIA
THRACE
CAUCASUS
Ilium
MYSIA
Pergamum
Winter 334/333
Gordium
Ancyra
May 334: battle near the Granicus
Alexandria
Eschate
HELLAS
Athens
Sardis
LYDIA
Ephesus
PHRYGIA
Miletus
PISIDIA
CAPPADOCIA
ARMENIA
Bactra
Maracanda
Nautaca
SOGDIANA
Bagai
Alexandria
CRETE
CYPRUS
Taurus
Nov. 333
Issus
Nisibis
MESOPOTAMIA
Oct. 331 decisive battle
Gaugamela
MEDIA
Alexandria
BACTRIA
Alexandropolis
PARTHIA
Zadracarta
Hecatompylos
Alexandria
Caspian Gates
Alexandria
Byblos
Thapsacus
Emesa
Palmyra
Ecbatana
Sidon
Tyre
Damascus
Taken after 7 months'
siege, summer 332
Prophthasia
Autumn 330
Alexandria
ARACHOSIA
Alexandria
Jerusalem
Babylon
331
Susa
Alexandria
Gaza
3 June, 323: Alexander
dies in Babylon after
10 days' illness
Persian
Gates
Pasargadae 324 end of the
march of conquest
Oasis of
Ammon
EGYPT
Memphis
Persepolis
Destroyed winter 331
GEDROSIA
Alexandria
Dec. 325 meeting
with Nearchus
Pattala
Indus
Route taken by the fleet under Nearchus

1

2

IN THE HANDS OF THE ASSYRIANS

Seen from the point of view of world politics Israel and Judah during the two centuries following the division of the kingdom formed part of the group of small states between the Euphrates and the Brook of Egypt which were perpetually warring with each other. In the east lay Edom, Moab, and Ammon, all formerly part of David's kingdom and independent after the division; to the north was Damascus, also once under David's rule, and farther north was Hamath. In the west were the Philistine cities with, to the north, Tyre, which dominated the coast up to Mount Carmel, Sidon, etc. We do not possess many details concerning this perpetual bickering. The fullest accounts in the Bible concern the wars between Israel and Damascus and only in so far as they form the background to the stories of Elijah and Elisha. The former strongly opposed the paganism which had penetrated the new capital of Samaria. Tirzah, which Omri abandoned in the sixth year of his reign and where archaeologists have found imposing but unfinished foundations just below the surface of the tell (→ 36, foot), lay at the head of a valley which opened southeastwards and formed a good link with Transjordan (→ 105, top). Under Omri, however, most of it was lost to Mesha, king of Moab, who records this on his famous stele. Anyone with a knowledge of Biblical Hebrew can read this unique remnant of Moabite literature (a convincing proof of the strong link between Israel and Moab, see p. 63) in which Mesha gives an account of his conquests in Israel north of the Arnon. Partly in order to present a stronger front against Damascus Omri chose his new capital so as to have good lines of communication with Tyre. His son Ahab married a princess from this city. This marriage heralded the large scale introduction of paganism that aroused the protest of Elijah. Ahab continued the struggle against Damascus, a struggle for commercial interest and the possession of Gilead with its citadel Ramoth-gilead in northern trans-Jordan. As we know from Assyrian sources fighting ceased for a time in 853.

Israel had long known that the old spirit of conquest once again prevailed in Assyria. It had also heard of the terrible methods employed by Ashurnasirpal (883–859) in his destruction of the small Aramaean states of Mesopotamia. In the name of the god Ashur, who wished to possess the whole world, his son Shalmaneser III (858–824) had added to the regions already conquered and extremely well organised by his father. He had penetrated into Cilicia and in 854 turned his armies towards the south. Near Qarqar on the Orontes, however, he was met by twelve allied kings whose names he gives, together with the contingents they brought with them. Ahab of Israel is companionably listed next to Hadadezer of Damascus! Shortly afterwards, however, they are again fighting among themselves, especially when the Assyrian menace seems to have lessened. In 841, Jehu, of whom we know so much from the stories about Elisha, the prophet who supported him in his policy, had to pay tribute to Shalmaneser who recorded this fact upon his

6½ft. high black obelisk, now in the British Museum. A detail from this obelisk (→ 108) shows Israel's king (with a pointed cap), prostrating himself before the Assyrian ruler who is pouring a libation. His gods are represented by the symbols of Ashur and Ishtar, a winged sun and a star. On this occasion Damascus had also to pay tribute. When shortly afterwards Assyrian pressure lessened, Damascus fell upon Israel with renewed vigour. Israel's position was weakened by the fact that its relations with Tyre had been severed as a result of Elijah's protests. This struggle was brought to an end by Adad-nirari III (809–782) who dealt Damascus a crushing blow. After him, Assyria passed through a period of internal conflict. Both Israel and Judah reacted by flourishing mightily, ruled respectively by Jeroboam II (783–743) and Azariah (Uzziah) (781–740). During the latter's reign the southern kingdom grew prosperous. Lost territories were reconquered, the ring of fortresses around Jerusalem was extended and made stronger, and the army was reorganised. In addition to these military activities methods were introduced to improve farming and stock-breeding. Yet even before these kings had gone to rest with their fathers the apparently somnolent giant in the north awoke once more.

Tiglath-pileser, the greatest ruler in Assyrian history, came to the throne in 745. He inaugurated the deportation system, by which, if it had not already been exterminated, the population of a conquered city was transferred to another part of the empire and replaced by colonists from still other regions. In this way he sought to kill the nationalism of the conquered peoples and to prepare an empire in which everyone would feel at home everywhere while being everywhere subject to members of the small, proud, nation of Assyria.

In 738 Tiglath-pileser began a series of campaigns against the west. In 734 he applied the deportation principle to a large section of Israel. His successor, Shalmaneser V, began a siege of Samaria. It was conquered in 721 by Sargon II and the inhabitants deported. This meant the end of the kingdom of the ten tribes. Under Sennacherib (705–681), Jerusalem barely escaped destruction. Judah might still survive, but for how long? Opposite is shown an illustration of the 'Assyrian method' found on a relief from Nineveh. While engineers tear down the outer walls of the city flames are already leaping from the citadel and the city gate. The last booty-laden soldiers have just passed through it (see p. 123) followed by a comrade driving two civilians before him. Below, a view of the army camp with soldiers and sutlers carousing. On page 112 is shown a reconstruction drawing of Dur Sharrukîn, Sargon's new capital on the site of the present-day Khorsabad, with, below, King Ashurbanipal hunting. The latter is a sample of the Assyrian mastery in the art of relief, especially in the depiction of animals. Covered battering rams on wheels (→ 113, top), the precursors of our tanks, were used to storm the walls. Above one sees inhabitants impaled upon stakes and others begging for mercy from the towers. There is also an officer (in a long skirt) drawing a bow, with a soldier next to him holding a shield taller than a man; behind them is a similar group. Below (→ 113, foot) is the picture of a group of deported inhabitants with Assyrian soldiers.

THE PROPHETS

Even the briefest survey of Israel's history cannot fail to mention the remarkable and, in the end, inexplicable phenomenon of Israel's prophets. Everyone remembers from the stories about Saul how, while searching for his father's asses, he meets a band of prophets in a state of exaltation and how he is carried away with them. This happens again later and afterwards Saul spends a day and a night naked upon the ground. A closer reading of these old tales reveals that this class of people who worked themselves into a state of trance with the help of song and dance in a way that we perhaps find difficult to accept, were honoured in Israel as one of the means by which Yahweh might reveal himself. It is openly told of the great Elisha that he needed a zither player to attain the state of trance in which he transmitted the will of Yahweh. We are also told that one of Jehu's officers, speaking of a prophet of Elisha's circle, exclaimed: 'Why has this madman come to you?' King Ahab had 400 such prophets in his service and their manner of obtaining for the king a revelation in God's name concerning for example the outcome of a projected campaign will probably not have been very different from the way in which the prophets of Baal tried to extort a sign from their god upon Mount Carmel. We now know that this sort of prophecy was also known in the lands around Israel and that some kings had included prophets in their court. The remarkable thing with Israel is that time and again such groups produced men who knew, in a manner difficult to describe but with complete certainty, that the God of Israel spoke to them and appointed them to be his spokesmen. Such people are found throughout the whole period of the monarchy, from Nathan, who voiced God's displeasure over David's shameful act, to the prophet Uriah who spoke in the same spirit as Jeremiah against the 'false' prophets and paid for this outspokenness with his life. They include too the 'writing prophets', so called because their words are handed down in the Biblical writings named after them. In former centuries they were involuntarily considered as theologians of a sort, gifted in addition with the ability to give particulars of the distant messianic future.

The end of the last century, however, brought a change in this manner of thinking. A careful analysis of the prophetic books showed that they had been composed long after the death of their supposed authors. They comprised fragments of their preaching, handed down orally and in writing and filled out with various texts, some of a much later date. A second reason was that modern man, with his sense of historical development and his interest in the personality of each individual, gained more understanding of the situation in which each prophet played out his rôle and the manner in which, in an entirely personal manner, he voiced the message of his God. It was noticed that the public activity of most of the 'writing prophets' coincided with periods of national crisis. The outline on the

The Prophets / The kings of Judah and Israel — chronological chart

THE PROPHETS ('Writing Prophets' in white on black)	attacks from EGYPT	(year)	The kings of JUDAH and ISRAEL	attacks from MESOPOTAMIA
Nathan, Gad			David / Solomon	*italics = usurper*
		950		
			(Disruption 931)	
Ahijah	Shishak (Sheshonq) →		Rehoboam / *Jeroboam I*	
			Abijam, Asa / Nadab, Baasha	
Jehu		900		ASSYRIANS
			Elah / *Zimri*, *Omri*	Ashurnasirpal III 883-858
Elijah			Jehoshaphat / Ahab	
Elisha		850		Shalmaneser III 858-824 ←(battle of Qarqar 854)
			Joram, Ahaziah (*Athaliah*), Joash / Ahaziah Joram, *Jehu*	←(tribute of Jehu 841)
				Shamshi-adad V 824-810
			Joahaz	Adad-nirari III 810-782 ←(tribute 805)
		800		
			Amaziah / Joash	(8 weak kings)
			Uzziah / Jeroboam II	Shalmaneser IV 781-772
Jonah				Ashurdan III 771-754
AMOS HOSEA		750		Ashur-nirari 754-746
ISAIAH			Zechariah	←*Tiglath-pileser III* 745-727
			Jotham / *Shallum Menahem*	←
			Ahaz / Pekahiah *Pekah*, Hoshea	←Shalmaneser V 727-722
			Hezekiah / deportation without return	Sargon II 721-705
	Tirhakah →	700		←Sennacherib 705-681
			Manasseh	Esarhaddon 681-669
				Ashurbanipal 669-626
		650		
ZEPHANIAH			Amon, Josiah	CHALDAEANS
JEREMIAH Huldah				Nabopolassar 625-605 (destroys Nineveh 612)
NAHUM Uriah	Necho →			
EZEKIEL	Hophra (Apries) →	600	Jehoahaz Jehoiakim ← / Jehoiachin-Zedekiah	←Nebuchadnezzar 604-562
			deportation to Babylon	*Evil-merodach* 561-560, *Nergal-sharezer* 559-556, *Nabonidus* 555-538
DEUTERO-ISAIAH		550		PERSIANS
			return	Cyrus 550-529 (conquers Babylon 539)
HAGGAI			Sheshbazzar, Zerubbabel	Cambyses 529-521, *Darius I* 521-486
ZECHARIAH		500		
			Ezra, Nehemiah	

opposite page will, it is hoped, clarify this. Within the framework are the kings of Israel and Judah; to their right, the rulers of the kingdoms in Mesopotamia (the names in italics are mentioned in the Bible; the arrows indicate their principal actions). Immediately to the right of the date column are the rare actions originating from Egypt, and to the extreme left of the page the row of prophets with the names of the writing prophets in capital letters. Towards the end of the extremely prosperous reigns of Jeroboam II and Uzziah, favoured by the weakness of Assyria, we see the first 'writing prophets' appear. Prosperity had above all profited the rich merchants and officials; they considered this as a material consequence of Israel's election which they celebrated in the pompous religious ceremonies. They remained blind to the fact that their unjust treatment of the lower classes cried out for vengeance. In this crisis Amos the unbending herdsman from Tekoa, proclaimed ruin and deportation in the name of Yahweh who nowhere tolerates injustice and certainly not among the people he has chosen. 'Israel's moral decay is in reality faithlessness towards a true and honourable partner' cried Hosea shortly afterwards. This prophet, abandoned by his wife yet continuing to love her, saw in the coming disasters the expression of an offended love.

In 745 Tiglath-pileser ascended the throne of Assyria and at the outset occupied himself with setting his own country in order. When, after some years, it became known in Jerusalem what this man intended to do in the name of his god Ashur, and the shrewd envisaged with dismay the possibility that Israel might soon cease to exist (and with it the dominion of Yahweh?), the well educated and gifted Isaiah underwent in the temple of Jerusalem his wellnigh shattering experience of the most holy God of Israel, who is the unique, the only Lord, 'the' King. He dared then to announce that the world conqueror was no more than a stick caught up by the God of Israel from beyond the Euphrates to chastise His people. All the peoples of Syria and Palestine would shortly be faced with the possibility of annihilation or survival: among the people of Yahweh only those would survive who believed, that is, who trusted in him alone. The vertical stroke under Isaiah's name in our scheme indicates the length of his ministry. He lived through the destruction of Israel and Sennacherib's vain siege of Jerusalem. A century later, when the Babylonians had taken over the Assyrian empire and its deportation methods, the end dawned for Judah. Jeremiah, sensitive and lonely but in constant conversation with his God, saw the uprising under Josiah, the failure of all the latter's good measures (if Yahweh would only engrave his commandments in the heart of man!) and the end of Judah's existence as a nation. The exiles of 587 were received in Babylon by Ezekiel, the eccentric but influential saviour of the old faith in that distant land. When, around 550 B.C., the whole of Mesopotamia was in ferment over the mysterious but mighty power descending from the Persian highlands (new war, new policy, a new and universal religion!) there emerged from among the exiles the unknown poet of Isaiah 40–55 commonly called the second or Deutero-Isaiah, who profoundly and stirringly proclaimed the restoration of Jerusalem. Around 520 a group of returned exiles wandered disconsolately among the ruins of temple and city. Here was another crisis, and now appeared the prophets Haggai and Zechariah.

On careful study of their authentic utterances, each prophet is seen to have a distinctive, characteristic manner of speaking about God, determined as much by his education and temperament as by the circumstances in which he prophesies. Yet notwithstanding the originality of their style, strong resemblances can also be detected, not only because the later prophets build upon the preaching of their predecessors (the young Isaiah was familiar with that of Amos, Jeremiah with that of Hosea), but because they all stand upon common ground, the heritage of Moses. Half a century ago it was still customary to view the prophets as the fell opponents of all outward forms of worship and as the discoverers of the service 'in spirit and truth'. This opinion has since been rightly moderated.

Nowadays many even believe that it was precisely the religious ceremonies which, in a combination of rites, narratives, and song, had preserved the essential core of Yahwism, and which formed the starting point for the prophets of that reflection to which their inward experience impelled them.

Whoever journeys through Palestine as a pilgrim is reminded time and again of these great spokesmen of God. On his arrival in Haifa he sees in thought Elijah's servant standing upon the promontory of Carmel looking for the rain cloud (→ facing). The visitor who has climbed the Mount of Olives near the German hospital (→ 97 foot, No. 10) where the small locality of Nob is sited with some degree of probability, must immediately think of the stirring poem in which Isaiah describes the Assyrian march upon Zion (Is 10 : 28–34, perhaps the sequel of 5 : 26–29). For he sees before him some of the places of which Isaiah speaks (see the small map; places in Isaiah 10 have black dots: some of the sites are uncertain). Turn-

ing, he understands how, from Nob, where he now stands, the Assyrian could shake his fist threateningly towards the hill of Zion which he sees lying below (→ 97 foot, No. 1). From there it is not far to the small village of 'Anâta near which lies the tell of Jeremiah's birthplace, Anathoth (→ 120, top). Following a pipe-line downwards from here one comes to the brimming spring from which drinking water is pumped to Jerusalem (→ 120, foot). It was called Parah in Jeremiah's time and is perhaps the Perath (which usually means Euphrates) of Jeremiah 13 : 4–7. On the way back he may feel annoyance at a farmer who has muzzled his threshing oxen (→ 121, top) contrary to the spirit of the prophets as revealed in Deuteronomy 25 : 4. Yet he will remember other texts upon threshing, like the moving expression used by a prophet in exile when addressing his defeated people, 'O my threshed and winnowed one' (Is 21 : 10). Farther on two farmers are busily tossing the threshed grain into the air: the heavy grains fall back, the chaff is scattered in the wind (→ 121, foot). This work put the prophets in mind of the separation of the good and the wicked: so shall the divine winnower divide the chaff from the corn when He comes in judgment.

EXILE AND RETURN

In 587 B.C. Judah suffered the same fate as had overtaken Israel in 721: the destruction of its land and capital and the deportation of the ruling classes. The eloquent relief (→ 111) serves thus to illustrate both calamities. The detail facing shows the conquerors carrying objects from the city temple, a throne (for the divinity?) and a large jar for the public ceremonies, a striking illustration of what the Bible narrates concerning the stealing of the sacred jars (2 K 25 : 14; cf. Ezra 1 : 7). The significance of this robbery did not lie only in the material value of the objects taken. It meant above all that the god of the victors had conquered the god of the city. There are, however, radical differences in the material aspects of the two calamities. The attackers of 587 were the Chaldaeans under Nebuchadnezzar. In his numerous inscriptions this brilliant ruler never speaks of his military operations but only of his many expensive constructions for the benefit of gods and men — temples, towns, and irrigation works. If, however, Babylon provides but little information concerning the drama of Judah's fate, the Bible makes good the deficiency. Most details are supplied by Jeremiah's friend and biographer Baruch. They were supplemented in 1938 by the unexpected and moving testimony of the inscribed shards from Lachish (→ 54 top*).

The fact that the Bible recounts Judah's fate in such detail is, however, closely bound up with the most important difference between 721 and 587: the exiles of Samaria were swallowed up in the Assyrian empire and disappeared without trace, those of Judah clung together and overcame as a group the effects of their uprooting. The continued influence of Judah's more stable past and the leadership of men like Jeremiah and Ezekiel ensured that the destruction of the familiar background led only to an immeasurable strengthening of the ancient faith. In the fever of daily happenings the Judaeans had once scorned the prophets' warnings. What they had predicted had now come to pass. Thus their words bore weight and were indeed inspired by God and charged with power. But in that case this was also true of their promises concerning the 'remnant' who would return. The exiles zealously assembled all that remained of their prophecies, whether in the memory or already put down in writing. This was then read and commented upon as 'the Word of God', still operative in their time. Historical traditions too were carefully written down and edited. A new edition was made of the great chronicle of Josiah's time (see p. 58). Written as a national epic it could now be used in the national examination of conscience. The stirring poems of Deutero-Isaiah reveal the force of inspiration that could emanate from this reliving of the past. Elements of the magnificent Marduk liturgy in sacred Babylon, a city expanded by Nebuchadnezzar into the most brilliant metropolis of antiquity (→ 125*), were perhaps combined with purely Israelite data in this prophet's exposition of the treasures which the faith of Yahweh concealed. However this may be, during the year that followed Cyrus' rise to power (after 550) he fanned the smouldering fire of hope among the exiles and his profound vision of the perfect servant of God was couched in words in which, six centuries later, Jesus of Nazareth would see the expression of His Father's will. Less than a year after Cyrus had taken Marduk's city without a struggle he issued the famous edict which allowed the Judaeans to return to their country and to rebuild the temple at his cost. Then, in and around Jerusalem, laboriously, and under the watchful interest of the Persian kings, there came into being the 'post-Exilic community'. The foundations were laid by two princes of the house of David, Sheshbazzar and Zerubbabel, aided by Haggai and Zechariah. Fifty years later Ezra and Nehemiah returned from Persia with authority to adopt the measures which are recorded in their memoirs and which the Chronicler (see p. 58) combined with other documents in the books of Ezra and Nehemiah, to try to give a general account of the Return. With this the story ceases. We have practically no direct information concerning the period between 400 and 167 B.C. Archaeological data are also extremely rare (→ 127★). And yet, in these centuries, events occurred of immeasurable importance both for the writing of the Old Testament and for the later propagation of Christianity.

In learned priestly circles in Jerusalem the old story cycles of Yahwistic history (see p. 94) were supplemented by material of a later date and mostly ceremonious in character (e.g. Gn 1 and 17, Ex 25–31, 35–40, and Lv). Genealogical lists were added, ages and data serving as an ingenious chronology dating from the Creation (reckoned as 3761 B.C.). Thus in the fifth century there emerged 'the Law' (see p. 58) which had such a profound influence upon Jewish life and thought throughout the succeeding centuries. After this, earlier collections of prophetic writings were gathered into the present books, often supplemented by texts containing apocalyptic expectations (Is 24–27, Ezk 38–39) and new were added (Malachi, Obadiah, Jonah, Joel). The 'profane' proverbial 'wisdom' of earlier times (see p. 94) was practised in a more explicitly religious manner (Pr 1–9 as introduction to the earlier collections 10–22 and 25–29). An exceptionally gifted writer composed the book of Job, and existing collections of psalms were augmented by new poems, mainly songs of praise and ingeniously turned didactic verses.

In the meantime, under the tolerant Persian princes who ruled either from Susa or from the glittering new capital of Persepolis (→ 126★), the 'Diaspora' began, the dispersion of the Jews throughout the empire (not always peaceable, see the book of Esther). The principal areas of this movement were Babylonia, where the largest section of Judaean exiles had remained behind, and Egypt, whither many had fled after the disaster of 587. Excavations on the island of Elephantine in the Nile opposite Assuân (Hebrew *Sewêne*, the Syene of Ezk 29 : 10, 30 : 6, the most southerly city of Egypt) revealed the existence of an important group of Jews, mainly soldiers in the service of Persia, in this economically and militarily important frontier city. The copies found there of letters and contracts (papyri of Elephantine, see 131, top★: a folded and sealed document and a few lines of writing underneath) throw light upon the relations of the distant imperial government with the Jewish cult even in this outpost, and upon the contacts of this colony with the centre in Jerusalem.

THE JEWS IN THE HELLENISTIC WORLD

When, in 334 B.C., Alexander, who had set out at the age of 22 upon a retaliation expedition against the Persians, had broken the resistance of their naval base of Tyre (→ 18, foot*), he pressed on into Egypt which greeted him as a liberator. Inspired by his beloved poet Homer (*Od.* IV, 354) he founded the port of Alexandria opposite the island of Pharos (→ 132, top*). Then, strong in the conviction of his divine origin (facing, top*) the new Pharaoh set out for Mesopotamia. Darius III suffered a crushing defeat. Towards the end of 331 Persepolis fell as sacrifice to the accumulated hate of many generations of Greeks (→ 126*). But Alexander wanted to go even farther, to the mighty sea that washes the shores of the world. When, four years later, in the strange land of India, his troops refused to advance farther eastwards, he had covered about 11,000 miles, fighting, conquering and founding new cities after the Greek model. Back in Babylon after a wearying retreat, the 33 year old conqueror died (13 June, 323), full of plans for the organisation of his vast empire and for even more ambitious expeditions.

The Jewish community in Palestine was not directly affected by this young phenomenon. After the long drawn-out wars among his successors, called the Diadochi, the coastal region fell, *ca* 300, to the Ptolemies who ruled from Alexandria. The Seleucids, however, who afterwards had their capital at Antioch on the Orontes, claimed to be the lawful rulers. Palestine thus was the apple of discord between 'the kings of the north and the kings of the south' (see Dn 11, → facing, foot*).

Issus

ANTIOCH
Residence
of the
Seleucids

N

Seleucia

Laodicea
Apamea

Arados
(Arvad)

Tripolis

Byblos

Berytus
Damascus
Sidon
Paneion

Tyre

Ptolemais   Scythopolis
(Acco)   (Beth-shan)

Samaria

Joppa   Philadelphia
              (Rabbah of
              the Ammo-
              nites)
              Jerusalem
Ashkelon
Gaza

Raphia

MEDITERRANEAN SEA

ALEXANDRIA
Residence of the
Ptolemies

Sais
Tanis
Mendes   Pelusium
Naucratis

0   25   50   75 miles

Petra

If at first the replacing of the Persian sovereigns by Greek conquerors meant for the Jews of Jerusalem only a change of tax collectors, gradually their attitude towards the new culture became for them a matter of principle. Long before Alexander, elements of Greek civilisation had penetrated deep into the Persian empire, borne there by merchants, mercenaries, and artists. For example, the coins struck *ca* 400 B.C. in the province of Judah, part of the Fifth Satrapy, followed the Attic model and bore the image of Athene's owl (→ 127*). The new rulers, however, propagated the Hellenistic culture in a positive manner. Local gods were identified with Greek deities, and this was tolerated: the Syrian Baal-shamem, 'lord of the heavens' became Zeus, as did the Amon of Thebes in Egypt, where the talented Ptolemies revived the old culture (→ 132, foot*). In Palestine the 'benefactors' (→ 133*) rebuilt old cities in the new style: Rabbah of the Ammonites became Philadelphia, Acco became Ptolemais. The educated people there spoke Greek, met in gymnasium and hippodrome, and were versed in the philosophy of the day.

But this way of life was difficult to reconcile with the precepts of the Law and Yahweh tolerated no identification with Zeus. Soon the Jewish community was split into two groups: the moderns, who wished to adapt the old faith to the new culture (these included many members of the upper and priestly cla ses), and the conservatives who thought that their ancient heritage could only be preserved by a complete rejection of all Hellenistic influence (like the writer of the book Sirach or Ecclesiasticus, *ca* 190 B.C.). Between these two extremes were the doubters and sceptics (including perhaps the writer of Ecclesiastes), while in Egypt the old Hebraic books were translated into Greek. In 198 B.C. the great Antiochus III (→ 128 foot, right*) brought Palestine finally under the dominion of the Seleucids. His son, Antiochus IV Epiphanes, who considered himself as an incarnation of Zeus (→ 133, 1st and 2nd from the top*) aroused the conservative party to revolt when he attempted to force them to adopt the Greek way of life and in 167 erected a statue of Zeus Olympius (perhaps made in his own likeness) in the temple of Jerusalem. The book of Daniel in its present form appeared during these years of crisis. The stories concerning this hero, assisted in so spectacular a fashion by the God of Israel in his revolt against pretentious rulers (Dn 1-6), were no less encouraging to the members of the resistance than the visions which were granted to him (Dn 7-12). These visions breathed the conviction that God had foreseen everything and was making ready to destroy utterly the fourth empire which, following upon those of the Babylonians, Medes, and Persians, had dared to launch a direct attack upon Yahweh himself. After this He alone would rule in the nation of the saints represented by a mysterious figure 'like a Son of Man'.

In the first book of Maccabees, written *ca* 100 B.C. and surviving only in a Greek translation, one can find a reliable account of the revolt and actions of the leaders, Judas (166-160) and his brothers Jonathan (160-143), and Simon (142-134). This book also reveals how the movement, at the outset purely religious, was soon dominated by political aspirations.

UNDER THE ROMAN EAGLE

The great Antiochus III (223–187 B.C.) who had given asylum to Rome's arch-enemy, Hannibal, was crushingly defeated in 189 by Scipio Africanus in Asia Minor (near Magnesia, northwest of Smyrna). He was killed when he went to plunder old temples in Mesopotamia in order to be able to raise the heavy tributes exacted by Rome. His son Seleucus IV was under the same pressure and sent Heliodorus to Jerusalem to rob the Temple (2 Mac 3: 7ff., cf. Dn 11 : 20). His other son, Antiochus IV, had spent fourteen years as a hostage in Rome, before being released in 176 B.C. He went to stay in the cultural centre of Athens, but left in 175 to seize the throne of his murdered brother Seleucus. He gained victories against the Ptolemies but when, in 168, he was on the point of annexing their kingdom to his own, he and all his troops were haughtily sent away from Egypt by the Roman consul Popilius Laenas. He departed to work off his rage on Jerusalem (cf. Dn 11 : 30).

The power of Rome prevailed at both ends of the coastal region, and it is thus understandable that the Maccabaean leaders should have turned to Rome for friendship and support in their struggle against the Seleucids. The author of the first book of Maccabees, who wrote his work in the classical Hebrew of Judges and Kings out of love for the great past which he thought now lived again, mentions these envoys to Italy with satisfaction. He evidently did not recall what – in that same great past – Isaiah thought of Hezekiah's embassies to Egypt for help against the Assyrians (Is 30 and 31). Devoted to the dynasty of the Hasmonaeans (as the successors of the Maccabees are usually called, in imitation of Josephus), he sees in them the revival of the old kingship (cf. the closing sentence of his book with 1 K 14 : 29). Their rule, however, reposed upon a different and too narrow basis. For the Maccabaean brothers were supported by only a section of the people, the devout, who followed the Law. The higher classes and many priestly families adopted the new culture and accepted the Seleucid rulers (cf. p. 130). When we read (in Josephus) that John Hyrcanus (135–104) undertook successful campaigns in Transjordan and against Samaria and that he forced the Idumaeans in the south to adopt the Jewish religion and circumcision, we must not think of campaigns like those of David and Josiah. John's army consisted mainly of pagan mercenaries and their leader behaved almost like a pagan ruler. Those who still were faithful to the Law rejected him, and some went off to live near the Dead Sea (cf. p. 146). During this time arose the party of the Pharisees, strongly opposed to the Sadducees, members of the old priestly families who, from the time of Jonathan Maccabaeus, had rebelled against the fact that he and his successors had assumed the office of High Priest.

Aristobulus (104–103), who murdered some of his blood relations and forced Judaism upon the Ituraeans in the north, was succeeded by his brother Alexander

Jannaeus (103–76. See → 133 left, foot*), who conquered nearly the whole of Palestine and the Transjordan. But he used his pagan mercenaries against his own people and made himself especially hated among the Pharisees. His widow Alexandra (76–67) restored their influence in the government and appointed her feeble son Hyrcanus High Priest. After her death the latter came into conflict with his energetic younger brother Aristobulus who had the support of the malcontents, notably the Sadducees and the army commanders. On the advice of Antipater, the father of Herod the Great, Hyrcanus sought the support of the Nabataeans who began to exercise considerable power from their capital Petra (→ 138*). Aristobulus, with the Sadducees and the pagan mercenaries, was engaged in fighting against his brother Hyrcanus, with his Pharisees and the Nabataean army, when word came that the Roman commander Pompey had arrived in Syria to annex what remained of the Seleucid empire for Rome (64 B.C.). What followed then was significant. Among the envoys who paid their respects to Pompey were three from Judaea: one from the energetic Aristobulus and his Sadducees with a request for intervention; one under the guidance of Antipater to ask help for Hyrcanus and the Pharisees; and one from the common people begging the Roman to put an end to the rule of the Hasmonaeans. This scene is significant in showing the rapid decay of the Maccabaean house and also characterises the decades that followed: anyone wishing to gain or retain power in Judaea must first obtain the favour of Rome.

Pompey recognised Hyrcanus as High Priest (63–40) but drastically curtailed his power. In 40 the Parthians, Rome's strongest enemy in the east, invaded Syria and Palestine, deposed Hyrcanus and replaced him by Antigonus (40–37), the son of his old enemy Aristobulus. Herod, who had previously shown himself as crafty in intrigue as his father Antipater, then went to Rome, convinced Antony and Octavian of his rights, and was made king of Judaea in 40 B.C. He had, however, to conquer his kingdom himself. After a subject visit to Antony who in the meantime had left for Syria to repel the Parthians, he obtained Roman troops and with them took Judaea and Jerusalem, where he had all his enemies put to death. At the outset of his reign (37 B.C.) Herod had to employ all his diplomatic talents to retain the confidence of the triumphant Antony on the one hand, and on the other to resist the intrigues of the latter's mistress Cleopatra (→ 133) who was trying to obtain Syria and Palestine as the Pharaohs of antiquity and the first Ptolemies had done. After Antony's defeat at Actium (31 B.C.) Herod quickly changed sides and offered his allegiance and help to the victor Octavian who in 27 B.C. was granted the title *Augustus*, that is 'exalted', 'divine', *Sebastos* in Greek, the language spoken by cultured people in Rome. For the Romans were strongly Hellenised, and it is certain that the many edifices built by Herod in honour of his imperial benefactor (cf. p. 151) were in the Greek style, like the later temples of Palmyra (→ facing, detail of → 139, foot*) and Ba'albek (→ 139, top*), which give us some idea of Herod's buildings. By systematically putting to death every person who could possibly be regarded as a pretender to the throne Herod tried to make his position secure, and by visits to Rome he strengthened his relations with the most powerful man in the world.

VOICES IN THE WILDERNESS

During the turbulent years of the revolt of the Maccabees another group had emerged alongside those of the Pharisees and Sadducees, that of the Essenes. Flaviu-Josephus (*ca* 37–100 A.D.), the Jewish historian who spent fully 35 years of his life in Palestine and whose works are our most important source of information concerning the history of the Jews after the Maccabaean rising, speaks of them as already existing at the time of Jonathan (160–143). Probably as a reaction against the corruption in Jerusalem, these devout people sought above all outward and inward purity. They held all their goods in common and lived in poverty and in obedience to a superior chosen by themselves. They refrained from commerce and took no part in the bloody animal sacrifices, although they rigorously followed the Law of Moses. Remarkable for their white clothing, their peculiar practices (e.g. morning prayers facing the rising sun) and some not entirely Jewish doctrines, they are mentioned by the Alexandrian Jew Philo (*ca* 25 B.C. – A.D. 50) and by the pagan Pliny (*ca* A.D. 23–79). The latter confirms their connection with the Dead Sea and adds that they dwelt a little distance from the shore on account of the evil mists which rose from the sea. Since they are not mentioned in the New Testament or in any of the official Jewish records, they were neglected until recently, except for a few specialists in Jewish history. This suddenly changed in 1949 when it was revealed that scrolls had been found two years before in a

cave near the Dead Sea. There is now no magazine that has not devoted an article to the story of the remarkable finds: the shepherd boy throwing stones through a gap in the rock wall and, hearing a metallic sound, creeping through the hole and finding jars with written scrolls inside them; the further investigations in other caves and the excavation of the only visible remains of human habitation, the ruin of *Qumrân*. Yet although the details are now well known these publications usually devote little attention to the setting in which all this took place. The photographs in this book seek to illustrate this background. They can be studied with the aid of the facing outline map upon which their areas are indicated. On → 142 (foot), taken from an aeroplane above the Dead

Sea looking northwest, one sees the water (black) to the right and to the left the mountain wall with the plateau transected by the winter rains from the mountain range. The ruin of *Qumrân* stands upon the area above the rugged north side of this incision.

On → 142 above, taken from the edge of the mountain facing northeast (the water of the Dead Sea is here white), the rectangular ruin on the plateau is seen as a black patch. Above it are some of the diggers' tents with two more tents to the right. An indentation can be seen on the foremost spur: this is the enlarged entrance to cave No 4. The photographer of → 144 stood near the tent above it, to the right, thus having cave No. 4 in the foreground (note the camel grazing far below to the left!) and in the background the mountain wall from which he took → 142 (top). This spot can be found in the foreground of the aerial photograph → 143 which looks towards the south. From a point between the plateau and the shore of the Dead Sea (see 142, foot) the panorama of → 140–141 (top) stretches westwards: left, the plateau, behind it, and running its whole length, the rugged reddish-brown rock face. On the photo below a man points to the original opening, the small hole through which the Bedouin boy threw his stones, with such interesting results.

On investigating the ruin (facing, top, looking southeast), it was discovered that building began under Hyrcanus (135–104). The complex was destroyed, either by the Parthians in 40 B.C. (see p. 136) or by the earthquake of 31 B.C. (see the large crack in one of the cisterns → 148, foot) and remained a ruin until the beginning of our era. It was then restored and flourished until its final destruction by the Romans in A.D. 68.

The complex, with its large rooms (see → 148, top), was not a dwelling house. The people who used it apparently lived in caves and tents, and met there to eat and pray together and to copy their sacred books (→ 59*) while supporting themselves by the work of their hands. In 1958 outbuildings came to light near the *Fashkha* spring (see map), a sort of farm with workshops in which the inhabitants of *Qumrân* dried dates (the salt marsh, black on → 143, is very suitable for date palms), cured the hides of their cattle, and so on. A laborious investigation of the whole length of the rock wall (→ facing, foot) showed that ten other caves possessed the remains of manuscripts, most of them in a very fragmentary state (→ 149*).

Thus, thanks to the curiosity of a shepherd boy and the energetic intervention of professional archaeologists of many different nationalities, we have gained insight into the manner of life and thought of a group of Jesus' contemporaries, identical or very closely related to the Essenes of Josephus and Philo. The remains of their careful copies of the Biblical books are of inestimable value for our knowledge of the textual history of the Old Testament. Possibly even more important are their Biblical commentaries and their own writings which show how these Jewish contemporaries of Jesus, far from the bustle of the town, found a new interpretation of the ancient piety of the Pharisees and lived in tense expectation of the absolute rule of God that was soon to come.

THE HIRELING AND THE GOOD SHEPHERD

Pagan contemporaries called King Herod (37–4 B.C.) 'the Great'. He was undoubtedly a capable ruler and promoted agriculture, trade, and industry. With keen insight he had one of the few anchorages on the coast enlarged to form the excellent port of Sebastos, and built a completely new town, Caesarea, the 'imperial', which was soon to become the real capital of Judah. He adorned the large hill of Samaria (→ 105, foot) with a magnificent city which, again out of gratitude to Augustus (see p. 136), came to be called Sebaste. At its highest point a temple was built in honour of the emperor (→ 157, top★). Outside Palestine, in Tyre, Damascus, Antioch, Rhodes, and even Athens he built temples, porticos, and colonnades.

He was, however, hated by his subjects, partly on account of the heavy taxes he imposed to pay for all this magnificent display, but especially by those who lived by the old traditions. To begin with, Herod was not a real Jew, but a descendant of the ancient Edomites whose name had become almost synonymous with 'arch enemy of God'. If David of Judah was once taken from his flocks in order to care for God's people and to rule them in the name of God, the prototype of the good shepherd (Ezk 34 : 16), this intruder, Herod, ruled in the name of the Romans who had given him his power. He was only able to maintain his authority with the help of Roman mercenaries, an uncircumcised rabble from all the countries of the world. Scarcely had he ascended the throne than he audaciously took control of the office of High Priest to which he appointed unworthy candidates whom he deposed and murdered whenever it suited his ruthless policy.

In order to gain the favour of his pious subjects Herod not only built a magnificent enclosing wall about the highly venerated burial cave of Abraham near Hebron (→ 157, foot★), but began a grandiose restoration and extension of the Temple in Jerusalem. He expanded the building surface into the enormous terrace which even now compels admiration (→ 166, top). One must imagine it covered with a shining white main building whose roof was overlaid with gold leaf, and surrounded by grandiose colonnades. But higher than the temple terrace and built before it was, stood a fortress, the Antonia, called after Herod's former Roman friend, and higher still, in the upper quarters of the town, was his palace with its three famous towers. For the king, by nature suspicious and jealous, knew that he was hated, and built himself fortresses even outside Jerusalem. He restored some of the mountain fortresses of the Hasmonaeans, preferably in the inaccessible region around the Dead Sea. Among these were Masada, Machaerus (→ 34, top), and Hyrcanium (→ 34, centre). He also built new citadels, such as the Herodium southeast of Bethlehem (→ 162★), where he was buried.

At this time Jesus was already born. The pilgrim who visits Bethlehem for the sake of Him, the Good Shepherd, looks down over the little town upon the abandoned tomb of Herod the Great – the wicked hireling (→ 34 foot★).

HEROD THE GREAT
Ruler of Palestine 39-4 B.C.
Augustus divided this region among Herod's three sons

ARCHELAUS (Judaea and Samaria)	**HEROD ANTIPAS** (Galilee and Peraea)	**PHILIP** (Ituraea, Trachonitis, etc.)

AUGUSTUS
Quintilius Varus

Birth of Jesus
6 B.C.

Volusius Saturninus
Quirinius

Coponius 6-9

M. Ambibulus 9-12

Annius Rufus 12-15

TIBERIUS

Valerius Gratus 15-26

Pontius Pilate 26-36

John the Baptist
Preaching of Jesus

Passion and Death of Jesus
Community of Jerusalem

Vitellius
CALIGULA

Marcellus 36-37
Marullus 37-41

granted to
Agrippa I

granted to
Agrippa I

Death of Stephen
Paul becomes a Christian

Petronius
CLAUDIUS

AGRIPPA I 41-44

Herod of Chalcis

Community in Antioch
James beheaded, Peter
taken prisoner

Vibius Marsius
Cassius Longinus

Cuspius Fadus 44-46
Tiberius Alexander 46-48
Ventidius Cumanus 48-52

Agrippa II
of Chalcis

Paul's first journey

Assembly in Jerusalem
Paul's second journey
1 Th   2 Th

Ummidius Quadratus

Antonius Felix 52-60

NERO

Agrippa II
Trachonitis, etc.

Paul's third journey
*Ph ?   1 Co   Gal
Ro   2 Co*
Paul captured in
Caesarea, taken to
Rome

Corbulo
Cestius Gallus

Porcius Festus 60-62
Albinus 62-64
Gessius Florus 64-66

Agrippa II

Col   Philem   Eph

Mucianus
GALBA etc.
VESPASIAN

Jewish uprising
Jerusalem destroyed
by Titus

*1 Ti   1 Tit
Mk   2 Ti*
Martyrdom of Peter
and Paul
*Mt ?
Lk-Ac?*

Judaea an imperial
province,
legates
Josephus writes
History of the Jewish War

TITUS
DOMITIAN

Josephus writes
Jewish Antiquities

NERVA
TRAJAN

*Rev   2 and 3 Ep of Jn?
Jn   1 Ep of Jn*

THE GOSPELS:
BACKGROUND AND COMPOSITION

The plan on the opposite page is intended to do two things: to give a simplified survey of the complicated political history which forms the background of the Gospels and of the Acts, and to form the basis for a short discussion on the special character of these chronicles. At the extreme left of the page are the Roman emperors in capital letters, for their will ruled the world of politics. The names in smaller print found between them are some of the legates who governed Syria in their name and also kept watch on the course of events in Palestine. The list in the middle is headed by Herod the Great.

After his death in 4 B.C. Augustus divided his territory among three of his sons whom he had not murdered: Archelaus, Herod Antipas, and Philip. The first ruled Judaea and Samaria as ethnarch ('ruler of the people', less than 'king' but the ordinary man made no distinction, Mt 2 : 22). He ruled badly (cf.Lk 19 : 12, 14) and was banished in 6 A.D. His territory then fell under governors, procurators, and the supervision of the legates in Syria. Herod Antipas ruled as tetrarch ('ruler of a fourth part', a worn-out title for rulers of small areas) much longer than his brother. Having come under suspicion in Rome he was banished to Lyon in A.D. 39. Philip, the best of the three, died childless in 34. His tetrarchy first came under Syria, but one of Herod's grandsons, Agrippa, educated in Rome, by playing his cards cleverly, was successful in obtaining it from Caligula who also gave him Antipas' region in A.D. 39. In 41 he received Judaea and Samaria from his friend the emperor Claudius, so that from 41 to 44 he ruled as king over all the lands of his grandfather. One of his brothers, Herod, was made king of Chalcis, in the Beqaʿ (see p. 10). On his terrible death, his son, Agrippa II, was too young to succeed him and Claudius appointed procurators to govern the greater part of his kingdom. Once again they formed a series of seven. In 48 Agrippa II was allowed to succeed his uncle in Chalcis and in 53 Claudius made him king of the regions formerly ruled by Philip and Lysanias (cf. Lk 3 : 1). Nero granted him a few more pieces of Galilee and Peraea in A.D. 64. This extremely Roman-minded king appears to have ruled until after A.D. 90. He was appointed inspector of the Jewish cult in Jerusalem. In 66 he tried to stop the senseless revolt but it continued to spread and led to the terrible destruction of Jerusalem in the year 70

After this Judaea was governed by Roman legates. The holy city was rebuilt in the Roman style and no Jew was allowed to enter it. This was a great blow to Jews and Christians everywhere, bud for the Christians this calamity had also a positive meaning. In confirmed their conviction that the history of Israel, meant as a preparation for God's universal dominion over all nations, was now at an end and that the lasting kingdom of God had really arrived. This conviction had lodged in the hearts of those who, forty years before, had been taught by Jesus of Nazareth and had seen him alive after His crusifixion and burial, and they had spread it throughout the empire, even in Rome itself. There, two of their leaders, Peter and Paul, had already paid with their lives for worshipping Jesus as the Messiah and the only true Lord of mankind.

The right-hand side of the table shows how matters stood around A.D. 70. Most of the letters of the New Testament have already been written and also the Gospel of St Mark. The Gospels of St Matthew and St Luke are accompanied by a query since it is not certain whether they were written before or after A.D. 70. At the bottom of the list stands the Gospel of St John, written towards the end of the century.

These four documents are called in Greek *evangelion*, meaning 'glad tidings'; they grew out of the proclamation of Christ's teaching. The first preaching in Jerusalem concerned the resurrection of Jesus: 'This man Jesus, whom you cruci-fied (this you all know well) was raised by God from the dead and is thus the Mes-siah, appointed Lord and Judge of all . . .'. For those not fully acquainted with the arrest and execution a sober account was given here which naturally, among the first preachers, scarcely differed. The same is true of the Bible texts chosen to elucidate the meaning of the Passion of the Messiah and of His Resurrection.

The case was slightly different when they came to write down what they re-membered of their contact with Jesus, of His words, His miracles, His sermons, and His parables. Each witness drew upon his store of memories in his own manner (everyone remembers experiences in a different way) and put them into words whenever they were called upon to describe Jesus as a man or tell of His mission. Naturally, in the course of much preaching and instruction of assis-tants these memories gradually assumed a more definite form and were written down. It is probable that as early as the fifth decade several of these collections were circulating in the then bilingual early Church, written both in Aramaic (including one by St Matthew, according to an early tradition) and in Greek. With the aid of such material Mark, the Greek adapter of Matthew, and Luke wrote the three Gospels named after them, remaining faithful to their sources yet retaining their own individuality as writers.

This process of composition had two main consequences. Since the Gospels (including the fourth, that of St John), are based upon a richly varied series of personal recollections, they give a more concrete picture of Jesus and of the im-pression He made upon His contemporaries than any critical biography in the modern manner could ever have done. Furthermore, since these reminiscences were formulated in order to further the proclamation of Jesus as the Messiah and Saviour of mankind they do not record such details as 'where' exactly, or 'when', often not even 'how'. Each Evangelist, although conscious of writing history, handles his material in his own way and with a freedom which nowadays amazes us.

The ways in which this method of composition affect our knowledge of Jesus' public life are discussed in the next chapter. First let us contemplate this photo-graph (→ facing*) of an Arabic village. It gives an excellent idea of the surroun-dings in which Jesus lived and worked until, a man of thirty, He entered upon the public scene.

JESUS OF NAZARETH

The lower photograph, facing, shows a section of present-day Nazareth, looking south. In the background is the plain of Jezreel. Here Jesus will undoubtedly have stood as a boy gazing out over the wide plain with its historic memories, towards the Carmel ridge farther west, a reminder to every Jew of Elijah the fiery warrior of God, eastwards to the mountains of Gilboa (→ 89, foot), celebrated by David in a song which every Jew knew by heart, and still farther east towards majestic Mount Tabor which will have reminded Him of Barak's fight for the God of Israel (→ 84). What lay directly before Him, however, was very different from what appears on the photo. Nazareth was then no busy pilgrimage centre, but an insignificant little village, mentioned neither by the Old Testament, nor by Josephus, nor by the Jewish Talmud. Other villages in Galilee (→ top facing and 155), give a better idea of what it must have been like than Nazareth itself. There Jesus assisted His father in the carpenter's shop which He later took over. The simple people among whom He lived are brilliantly sketched in his parables, of which it has rightly been said that no other literature of Roman imperial times gives such a lively picture of the daily life of the common people.

The nature of Jesus' inner life is strikingly indicated by St Luke who records Him, a twelve year old who has remained behind in the temple during a pilgrimage to Jerusalem, as saying to His parents: 'Did you not know that I must be about My Father's business?' (Luke 2 : 49).

When He was about thirty years old John's call to conversion and repentance reached Nazareth. Jesus heard it and left His family in order to be baptised in the winding Jordan (→ 161). It is no longer possible to determine exactly where this baptism took place: a Bethany 'beyond the Jordan' (Jn 1 . 28) is not mentioned anywhere else, and the place Aenon (the name means roughly 'regions of springs') where John baptised 'because there was much water there' and which lay near Salim (Jn 3 : 23) is also impossible to locate with certainty.

After a sojourn in the barren wilderness of Judaea (→ 162*), since that time a favourite region for Christian anchorites (→ 29*), Jesus proceeded to Galilee. There He began to preach that the kingdom of God was at hand, continuing in His own way the task of John the Baptist who at this time lay imprisoned in the fortress of Machaerus east of the Dead Sea (→ 34), as punishment for his outspokenness to Herod Antipas. Jesus preached mainly in the region around the Sea of Galilee (→ 164–165) shown on the photo from the west. In the foreground, on the coast with its delightful climate and medicinal warm springs lies Tiberias, the city founded between A.D. 17 and 22 by Herod Antipas to be the new capital of his tetrarchy and named after his overlord in Rome, Tiberius. In common with other devout Jews of this region, Jesus appears to have avoided this city which had adopted Hellenistic morals and manners. He was most at home (insofar as this word can be used in connection with Him) in Capernaum, about 6 miles farther north, now, apart from the synagogue, a heap of ruins like Chorazin and, on the northeast shore, Beth-saida. This town belonged to the tetrarchy of Philip and was rebuilt by him at the beginning of our era and named Julias, in honour of a daughter of Augustus.

In Capernaum lived Peter, Andrew, and the sons of Zebedee, the first disciples, who at a word from Jesus abandoned their little fishing businesses in order to follow Him, such was the strength of His fascination for them. For the coming reign of God, seen by John the Baptist as judgment, sentence, and the destruction of the wicked, was characterised by Jesus as the revelation of the merciful love of God, whom, in an incomparable way, He called His Father. Still more, He spoke of this revelation as having already begun in his own person and confirmed this by limiting Satan's domain wherever He thought good: He drove out devils, healed the sick, and even raised the dead to life. For, wherever the living God is obeyed completely and rules absolutely, sickness and death lose their power. Although we know little of the sequence and routes of Jesus' journeys, His stay in the distant regions of Tyre and Sidon appears to coincide with a crisis in His Ministry. After Peter's profession of faith in the country of Caesarea Philippi and the Transfiguration on the Mount (nearby Mount Hermon? or Mount Tabor?), He began to prepare His disciples for the suffering He would have to undergo in Jerusalem and which would definitely ratify the revelation of God's kingship.

Before this time Jesus had journeyed to Jerusalem for the great feasts only, time and again to come up against the lack of comprehension of the leading circles, as in the mysterious district of Dalmanutha-Magadan. Sometimes in the course of these journeys He passed through Samaria where, at the well of Jacob near Shechem (→ 86, 69) He once spoke with a woman drawing water (see → 163, top), and sometimes through the eastern part of the Jordan valley which formed part of Peraea. The frontiers of the various territories given on Map 8 (facing p. 168) obviously did not prevent freedom of movement. His last journey also lay through Peraea, to the city which enjoyed the lugubrious fame of being fatal to prophets. There He boldly appeared in the temple (→ 166, top★) which was still being built, and openly prophesied its destruction. In the evenings He walked through the deep valley of the Kidron (166, foot★) or to His friends in Bethany or to the Garden of Gethsemane at the foot of the Mount of Olives. For the site of these and other places from the story of the Passion, see the map of Jerusalem (facing p. 85), to be compared with the aerial photographs (→ 96, foot and 97). The site of the Pavement or Gabbatha (see 166, top) is extremely doubtful and consequently the route of Jesus' wearying Way of the Cross through narrow and often stepped streets (→ 167, right★). We know for certain, however, where Calvary stood. This rise in the ground, commonly called Golgotha, 'skull', lay in Jesus' time just outside the city gate where many roads met. Nowadays this piece of rock and the tomb a little farther up hewn out in a garden (→ 168★) are covered by a not very beautiful complex of churches, the first goal of every Christian on arrival in Jerusalem. For the Pharisees the Jesus affair was definitely closed on that Friday: had God been with this man He would certainly have saved him from death.

PALESTINE IN THE GOSPELS AND ACTS

 Provincial boundary (approximate)
aba Modern Arabic name

Caesarea Philippi Mt 16 13

PHOENICIA

GAULANITIS

Ptolemais Ac 21:7

GALILEE

Main centre of the preaching of Jesus

Chorazin

Beth-saida (Julias)

Capernaum Mt 4 13

Cana Jn 2:1

Magdala

Lake of Gennes-ret

Kafr Kenna

Tiberias

Hippos

Nazareth Mt 2:23

TABOR

Nain Lk 7:11

Gadara

Abila

DECAPOLIS

federation of ten Hellenistic cities

Caesarea Residence of the Roman procurators Ac 10

Scythopolis

Pella

Sebaste the former Samaria

Salim(?) Jn 3 23

PLAIN OF SHARON

SAMARIA

Sychar Jacob's Well Jn 4

GERIZIM

Gerasa

Antipatris Ac 23:31

Alexandrium

Joppa Ac 9:11

Arimathea home of Joseph, a member of the council Mt 27:57

PERAEA
'beyond the Jordan'

Lydda Ac 9:32

Ephraim Jn 11:54

Philadelphia

Jamnia

Emmaus(?) Lk 24:13

Jericho

Ashdod Ac 8:40 (Azotus)

JERUSALEM

Bethany

Kh Qumrân

Ashkelon

Bethlehem

Mar Saba

J U D A E A

Herodium

DEAD SEA
also called the Asphalt Lake

Hebron

Machaerus Mk 6:14-26

Gaza Ac 8:26

Masada

Beer-sheba

I D U M A E A

0 5 10 15 20 miles

NABATA

8

THE TRAVELS OF SAINT PAUL

According to the Acts of the Apostles

First journey (13-14) ---- Second journey (15.36-18.22) ---- Third journey (18.23-21.15) ....

▼ Where preaching in synagogues is expressly mentioned

45 The dates of the beginning and end of the journey are not completely certain

As a prisoner to Rome (27-28)

Journeys planned but prevented

45 The dates so indicated was probably written in this city

Gal. The Epistle so indicated was probably written in this city

Antioch A.D. 45 The Holy Spirit intervenes at prayer for me Barnabas and Saul. A.D. 48 after quarrelling with John-Mark, Paul and Silas on his second journey. A.D. 52 Paul returns to Antioch and sets out on his third journey which ends in the prison at Caesarea in A.D. 57

'Healing of a cripple: "the gods have come down to us in the likeness of men".' the Jews stone Paul

Tarsus

First sermon in Antioch: example of Paul's preaching; reaction of Jews and Gentiles

Paul meets Timothy, his 'true child in the faith'

John, called Mark, deserts Paul

Paul is warned by a prophet: 'I am ready even to die'

After being almost lynched before the Temple, Paul is confined in a Roman barracks. A.D. 57-59 he addresses the people and is taken to Caesarea

Paul brought before the governor Felix by the Jews. A.D. 57-59 he is for two years in prison. His case comes before Festus and Agrippa. Paul speaks to Caesar, to Caesar he shall go. A.D. 59 sent as a prisoner to Rome

Binding of the Jewish magician; conversion of proconsul Sergius Paulus. From this point Saul and his company

Paul preaches here for two years, causing a rising of the silversmiths: 'Great is Artemis of the Ephesians'

Europe calls 'Come over ... and help us'

Paul bids farewell to the elders of Ephesus: 'You will see my face no more'

Paul preaches late into the night; a young man, overcome by sleep, falls to his death from a third storey window; Paul raises him to life and continues preaching

Paul proclaims the 'unknown God'; the Athenians mock and not accept the resurrection of the dead

'Not the wisdom of the Greeks but the folly of the cross.' Paul before Gallio

Paul warns that the journey will be perilous

For fear of running on the Syrtis the sailors lower the sails

Violent gales prevent the ship from entering the sheltered harbour

The ship's boat is hoisted aboard

All hope is abandoned; Paul predicts shipwreck; on his account God will save everyone on board

After drifting for fourteen days the ship founders; all are saved. A.D. 59-60 the winter is continued aboard the Twin Brothers

Mutiny of the crew is suppressed by the soldiers; the cargo of wheat is jettisoned

Paul stays here three days

'The Jews declare "These men have turned the world upside down"'

Paul stays at the house of Lydia; his song of praise in prison

'There we found brethren'

When Paul saw the brethren of Rome he took courage

Two years' imprisonment in Rome (A.D. 60-62) But the word of God is not fettered (2 Tim 2.9)

Col. Ph. Eph. and Philem.

2 Cor

1 and 2 Thess

Ro

Gal (and 1 Co)

'MY WITNESSES TO THE END
OF THE EARTH'

To Luke, a doctor from Antioch (→ 172, foot*) who became Paul's most faithful companion, we owe not only the third Gospel with its particularly sensitive portrait of the Saviour, but also that document which we know as the 'Acts of the Apostles' and which the author intended as a sequel to his Gospel. Some find it advisable to begin the reading of the New Testament with this book. The first chapters indeed give a stirring picture of the overwhelming impression which Jesus' resurrection made upon His disciples, transforming them from vacillating and fearful followers into courageous witnesses who knew themselves to be supported by an all-conquering power.

The various speeches of Peter recorded by Luke are so archaic in style and content that he must either have employed written sources or have been able to enter completely into the transports of the first days and months. However this may be, it is extremely profitable to compare these accounts of the first preaching see Ac 2,3,4 and 10, cf. 13) and to see for oneself how, relying on Old Testament texts, the disciples saw Jesus' resurrection as the seal of God upon His Ministry and how they considered these facts decisive for the whole of humanity and for every man, being the commencement of the long awaited kingdom of God. Taking this into account one becomes more easily reconciled to the fact that the Gospel stories concerning Jesus' resurrection and apparitions are so disconnected and on some points cannot even be reconciled with each other. Each evangelist obviously drew upon the traditions at his disposal and it is understandable that the recollections of the marvellous experiences of those days of profound emotion should have differed so strongly. The important fact is that all the people who first recounted and transmitted these stories belonged to the communities which we see springing up in the Acts: the link which bound these people together (and also painfully divided them from the Jewish community) was the conviction that God had raised his servant Jesus from the dead and, having raised him to his right hand, had appointed him Lord and Messiah, the Saviour of all mankind. They had either seen Him alive themselves or placed their trust in the testimony of those to whom He had appeared and to whom He had given His world embracing commission.

Luke devotes the second and larger part of his work to Paul. It is significant that this thoughtful writer, who is usually careful to avoid repetition, includes three detailed accounts of Paul's experience on the road to Damascus (in Ac 9, 22, and 26). This is evidently his way of expressing the immeasurable importance of this event for the young Christian church. Seldom, indeed, was anyone better equipped than Paul for the task that awaited him. Born at Tarsus in Cilicia of orthodox Jewish parents and sent to Jerusalem as a child to receive legal training as a Rabbi from masters who included the famous Gamaliel, he was familiar with the two main forms of Jewish life, of the Dispersion and of Jerusalem. By his command of

'Koinè' Greek, spoken by cultured people of these times, he was able to communicate with all the educated people of the empire. He had inherited Roman citizenship, a privilege that included all kinds of facilities and which even high-ranking officers were sometimes obliged to purchase at a considerable price. He was capable of quick and clear reasoning and elevated mystical contemplation. He had, in addition, an extremely agile mind, capable of experiencing a whole range of feeling within a few seconds. Paul had, from his youth, placed all these gifts at the service of his God. Even more than his colleagues he detested the followers of Jesus for he saw more clearly than they that this sect threatened the very foundations of the Jewish community, the heritage of God. He continued to hold this view until, near Damascus, it was made clear to him that in combating the supporters of Jesus he was fighting, not the enemies of his God, but the Messiah, the Christ for whom he had longed from his youth. If one reads Paul's letters in the light of the journeys which Luke records and in the order of their writing (the map facing p. 169 may be of help here) one sees how during this restless coming and going, through desolate mountain passes (→ 173), in battered little ships, and along endless roads (→ facing*), he penetrates deeper into the reality which is finally revealed to him upon the road to Damascus and in the Street called Straight (→ 172, top left).

It was not only the will to convey his message plainly and convincingly in the most diverse circles, among Jews and heathens, educated and illiterate, which impelled him to ceaseless reflection, but also the crises and defections of some of his community. The faithful of Thessalonica lead him to clarify the doctrine of the second coming of Jesus (who had died barely twenty years before) and the Jewish teachers in Galatia lead him to define more clearly the doctrine of justification by faith. The converts of the turbulent metropolis of Corinth (→ 172, top right) with their questions and disputes, draw from him some sublime pages, and during his two years' imprisonment in Rome the fallacies of the Colossians lead him to a consideration of the final consequences of Jesus' work for humanity and for the universe. Luke's work ends with the mention of this stay in Rome (61–63). Paul made other journeys after this, to judge from his letters to Timothy and Titus in which he draws up measures for the further organisation of his communities and charges these helpers with the preservation of the doctrine he has preached. He was beheaded in Rome probably ca A.D. 67; Peter had probably been martyred earlier.

By this time, however, Christianity had already obtained a firm hold within the Roman empire. Paul used by preference to work in the largest centres like Ephesus, the most important junction of sea and land routes on the coast of Asia Minor. There the silversmiths had rightly exclaimed that their great Artemis, the lewd goddess with her many breasts, would be 'deposed from her magnificence' (Ac 19 : 27, see 174, top left) if Paul were left in peace. In the place of these and other divinities, including the unknown gods which the people worshipped for fear some should be neglected, (Ac 17 : 23, see → 174, top right), Christianity proclaimed the God of Israel whose Temple in Jerusalem had been given up to destruction (→ 174, foot) because now, in Jesus His Son, He sought to take up His abode in the hearts of all mankind.

NOTES ON THE PLATES

The bold numbers are page numbers

11. The Jordan valley from a considerable height, looking NNW. To the right the valley of the Jabbok joins the Jordan valley proper. The latter shows dark on the photograph because of the dense undergrowth through which the river flows. The light patch a little to the left of the Jabbok mouth is *Tell ed-Dâmiyeh*, the tell of the city of Adam, where the waters of the Jordan were held back (Jos 3 : 16). The side valley on the left is the *Wâdi Far'ah*. At its head lies the tell of ancient Tirzah (see **105**, top, taken from the opposite direction). **12**. TOP: the port of Tripolis, an ancient Phoenician settlement where Arvad, Tyre, and Sidon each had their quarter, hence the Greek name 'triple city.' In the background the Lebanon. FOOT: Mount Hermon seen from the NE from the slopes of the Lebanon across the Beqa'. **13**. TOP: the most famous of the rare plantations of cedars remaining in the Lebanon. It lies 20 miles southeast of Tripolis and contains about 400 trees, some of which are more than 1000 years old. FOOT: at the edge of the cedar wood. **14**. Conquered Phoenicians cutting cedars for the Pharaoh. Right, four of the vanquished humble themselves before an Egyptian officer (not shown). Detail from a relief carved on a temple wall in Thebes (Karnak) by order of Seti I (1317–1301 B.C.). **17**. TOP: Mari on the Euphrates, for many centuries a flourishing trading centre, destroyed *ca* 1700 B.C. by Hammurabi, and accidentally discovered in 1933 by nomads who upturned a statue while digging a grave. It has subsequently been excavated in annual campaigns. The photograph, taken after the fourth campaign, shows in the background the famous royal palace with its 260 rooms, inner courts, etc. A collection of roughly 2,000 tablets with cuneiform writing was found, providing valuable information concerning the history and culture of this region. In the distance, the Euphrates. FOOT: the Tigris near *Jezîret Ibn Omar*, the ancient Bezabde, where Alexander the Great crossed the river twelve days before his decisive victory over the Persians near Gaugamela (2 Oct., 331 B.C.). At that time the Tigris flowed around the city at high tide, hence the alternative name of Gozarta, 'island' (Arabic: *jezîreh*). For a time the city was ruled by the chief Ibn Omar. Since 1929 the Turkish frontier, visible in the background, has run in front of the city with its ancient ramparts. Its Turkish name is Cizre. **18**. TOP: the island of Ruâd, 2 miles from the Phoenician coast. The important city of Arvad was situated here. FOOT: Tyre, once a mighty island city like Arvad, was taken by Alexander in 332 B.C. after a siege of 7 months, with the help of a causeway which linked the city permanently with the mainland and transformed it into a peninsula. **19**. Obelisks in an excavated temple at Byblos, testifying to Egyptian influence in this city. **20–21**. The oldest capital of Egypt, a little south of Cairo, was called *mn-nfr* on account of its beauty. The inhabitants of Israel shortened this to Moph or Noph, and the Greeks called it Memphis. Behind the palms which now grow where the city formerly stood, one sees on the edge of the western desert the famous stepped pyramid of the Pharaoh Zoser, *ca* 2600 B.C. **22**. TOP: the Nile somewhere between Cairo and Luxor. Note the sharp difference between the irrigated region and the sun-baked desert on either side of it. FOOT: the Nile near Luxor. The small town derives its name from the ruins of the 'city of Amon' (No-amon or No in the Bible, called Thebes by the Greeks) among which it is built and which the Arabian inhabitants called *el-Qusûr*, 'the castles'. A little farther north lies the small town of Karnak, near the ruins of the Amon temple. In the centre of the photograph, on the near bank, can be seen the great rows of columns of Rameses II, shown in close up on p. 71. On the west bank an arrow indicates the Valley of the Kings. Here Hatshepsut built her Temple of the Dead. **23**. TOP: the famous Valley of the Kings. Left of the centre, a dotted line indicates the spot where the processions entered the desolate valley. Every pharaoh of the New Kingdom had his burial chamber hewn in the heart of the mountains, which thus served as pyramids. Of the 60 known tombs, each reached by a long and often magnificently decorated corridor from the valley, three are visible on the photograph: near 1, the entrance of the long shaft to the tomb of Rameses II; near 2, that of Rameses VI; near 3 beginsthe passage to the tomb of Tutankhamon, the only one that escaped the attention of tomb robbers of former centuries. It was found almost intact in 1922 after years of searching by scholars who knew that it had still probably remained untouched. **23.** FOOT: in the foreground the Temple of the Dead of Queen Hatshepsut, with three ascending terraces, of which the second is the largest. In the background is a much older temple from *ca* 2000 B.C., with only one terrace. **24.** The Dead Sea from a great height, looking SSE. The dotted line indicates roughly the area of the photograph on p. 143. From the Jordan and smaller rivers like the Arnon this inland sea receives over 6 million tons of water per day. In normal conditions this would mean that the water would rise about half an inch every day, but the rapid evaporation in this hot, deep bowl between high rock walls prevents this. Because of the evaporation the water is very rich in minerals; it contains roughly 25 per cent of salts; see the pans for extracting salt near the Jordan estuary to the left. Fish brought down to the Dead Sea die within a few seconds. Called in the Bible the Salt Sea or Sea of the Plain, it was given the name of Dead Sea at the beginning of our era; only a miraculous stream flowing from God's Temple could render the water capable of sustaining life (Ezk 47 : 1–12). **27.** TOP: view of *Kafr Kenna*, a picturesque spot a few miles NE of Nazareth, considered since the 4th century to be the Cana of John 2 : 1. FOOT: from the towers of the basilica which crowns Mount Tabor (see → 84, foot) one sees to the west, over the Greek monastery and its annexes, the hills of Lower Galilee, where Nazareth lies hidden. **28.** TOP: the hill country of Judaea. FOOT: part of the desolate Negeb, the south country, looking east. In the distance, the valley of the Arabah running from north to south; behind, the highlands of the Edomites. **29.** TOP: the wilderness of Judaea at the level of Bethlehem. In the distance, the Dead Sea; behind, the mountains of Moab. FOOT: the fortress, exactly in the middle of the preceding photograph, stands near the tower shown upper right in this. They form part of the wall surrounding the monastery, built here against the side of the deeply indented Kidron valley by followers of Sabas, a Cappadocian who came here as a hermit in 478. Throughout the following centuries this monastery was famous as a centre of art and learning. **30.** The small village of *Jebeil* and the excavated tell of ancient Byblos. **33.** TOP: the tell of ancient Hamath surrounded by the houses of modern Hama. FOOT: the Orontes in Hama. The tell stands in the background. **34.** TOP: remains of the fortress of Machaerus, restored by Herod the Great. In the background, the Dead Sea, which lies 3,700 ft. lower, and behind, the steep mountain wall of the desert of Judaea. CENTRE: across the small valley of *el-Buqeia* one sees the citadel of Hyrcanium, built by John Hyrcanus and fortified by Herod the Great. From his hermitage, a few miles farther west (Mar Saba, see → 29, top) Sabas founded in 492, in the ruins of this fortress, a monastery which flourished until the 9th century. FOOT: a view of Bethlehem looking southeast. The arrow indicates the Herodium, the fortress which Herod built and intended as his tomb. **35.** TOP: the tell of Biblical Dothan, shortly after the first excavations in 1953. FOOT: the same tell from the side, scarcely recognisable as such. Left, nomad tents. **36.** TOP: excavators at work in Biblical Tirzah. FOOT: exposed foundations of Tirzah. **39.** Palestinian pottery. LEFT and FOOT: the oil lamp in the various stages of its development. In the earliest times an ordinary round dish was filled with oil and the wick placed across the edge. Then the potters curved the edge to hold the wick in position. Later the curve became more pronounced and, with the gracefully sloping sides, formed a sort of lip. RIGHT: six pots and jars. Particularly striking is the one on which is modelled a face with a large nose and a pointed beard (8 in. high, Hyksos period, from Jericho). Above and below, vessels from the Israelite period. The three specimens on the right date from the Middle Bronze Age (*ca* 2000–1600 B.C.); the lowest is Mycenaean in character and was probably imported. **40.** TOP: weather-beaten Phoenician sepulchral monuments near *Amrît*, a city on the coast founded by the inhabitants of Arvad (→ 18, top). These giant structures indicate the presence of burial chambers dug deep in the ground beneath. The monument to the right consists of a pedestal with lion figures at the corners, on which rests a cylindrical block, 23 ft. high, made from a single piece of stone. FOOT: section of a rock tomb from the Middle Bronze Age found near Jericho. The contents are now in the Rijksmuseum voor Oudheden in Leiden, arranged exactly as they were when found. **41.** TOP: the jars and dishes in which the ancient inhabitants of Palestine placed food for their dead are often found almost intact: *left*, a group of pottery dating from before 3000 B.C. *right*, a find dating from roughly 1800 B.C. CENTRE: people buried round a horse, probably from the Hyksos period, found near *Tell el-ʿAjjûl* south of Gaza. FOOT: in 1952 burial places dating from the time of Christ were found on the Mount of Olives near 'Dominus Flevit'. A large number of 'ossuaria', stone chests containing the bones of those who had first lain in a burial chamber (see → 168), came to light. The name of the deceased is often inscribed on these chests, sometimes in Greek, sometimes in Aramaic. On the Mount of Olives were found the names of Jairus, Martha, and Mary (→ 167, foot), Simon Bar Jonah, Jesus, Salome, Philo of Cyrene. RIGHT: two sarcophagi: the upper is a limestone ossuarium from the time of Christ; the name reads 'Salome, the wife of Lazarus'; below, a sarcophagus of baked clay from the 12th century B.C. found at Beth-shan. A face, ears, and arms are modelled on the lid. This type, also found in the Nile Delta and in the country of the Philistines, testifies to Egyptian influence in Canaan. **42.** Pyramid-shaped top of an obelisk in the ruins of the great temple of Amon at Thebes (Karnak). **47.** TOP: top of the 6½ ft. high pillar of black diorite on which King Hammurabi engraved a code of laws *ca* 1690 B.C. It contains 282 paragraphs as well as an introduction and a conclusion. Carried away from Babylon by the Elamites as a trophy, it was found in 1902 at Susa: *left*, the king, standing and respectfully carrying his right hand to his mouth; *right*, the sun god Shamash who sits on a throne representing a temple; his feet rest on a stool which symbolises a mountain range; the four pairs of horns on his head indicate his divinity. As protector of the law, Shamash hands the king a staff and a ring. FOOT: as a specimen of the cuneiform text the beginning of paragraph 25 is shown here. Each sign has the value of a syllable. Beginning at the top right the 8 columns read: *shum-ma i-na bît a-wi-lim/i-sha-tum/in-na-pı-ıkh-ma/a-wi-lum/sha a-na bu-ul-lı-ım/ıl-lı-ku/a-nu nu-mu -at/be-el bîtim*, which means 'if in a man's house/a fire/has broken out/and if some person/ who in order to put it out/has gone there/on the property/of the master of the house . . .', and Hammurabi continues, 'has cast his eyes and has taken the property of the master of the house, that man shall be cast into this same fire'. **48.** TOP: a clay 'nail', probably used as a wall decoration in the temples of south Mesopotamia. This specimen, from the De Liagre Böhl collection in Leiden comes from Lagash. The text informs us that the ruler of this city, Entemena (*ca* 2350 B.C.), has built a house for his gods and has designed the interior, and further that he has signed a pact of friendship with the ruler of Uruk (the Biblical Erech). CENTRE: letter from a Babylonian officer (the match serves to indicate the scale!) dating from the years before the destruction of the empire in 538. Mention is made of a certain Gubarru (*Greek* Gobryas) probably the person who played a part in the fall of Babylon. One also reads the names *nabu-kudurri-usur*, 'Nebo protect the landmark', spelled in the Bible Nebuchadnezzar (in some versions Nabuchodonosor) and *Nergal-shar-usur*, 'Nergal protect the king', who is mentioned in the Bible as a commander of Nebuchadnezzar at the conquest of Jerusalem in 587 B.C. under the name Nergalsharezer (Jer 39 : 3), and who later, in 559, became king of Babylon. FOOT: contracts concerning deliveries of corn, also from the De Liagre Böhl collection in Leiden; *left*, one of these contracts in its 'envelope'. The specimen on the right, being held beside the envelope, is dated in the 44th year of King Shulgi of Ur, *ca* 2000 B.C. Clay offered an indestructibility that modern paper cannot provide. When the small contract had been written and the names of the witnesses added before the clay was dry, it was enclosed in a layer of wet clay, the 'envelope', on to which the text was thus transferred, together with the names of the witnesses. The seals of the contractors were then affixed. If, after the signing of the contract one of them maintained that alterations had been made to the text, the judge had the envelope broken open and the original text appeared. **49.** In ancient Mesopotamia everyone of importance had his own seal, a small cylinder made of precious or semi-precious stone with a picture, usually religious, engraved on it and sometimes also a text. A hole was bored through it lengthways so that it could be worn on a chain round the neck. The owner rolled it across the wet clay of a written tablet by way of a signature On the envelope on page 48 two such imprints are visible, one at the top and one at the bottom. We show here a few specimens from the tens of thousands which are known to exist. They are the object of a special branch of archaeological study. *Above*, the sun god rising between the mountains. *In the third row*, two impressions from seals showing scenes from mythology: to the left is a ziggurat, to the right two people near the tree of life, with the serpent. *Foot*, a seal of precious green stone with rings of shell and a silver nob; to judge by the picture it probably belonged to a priest in charge of a temple herd. The second seal from the top was found at Beth-shan and is characteristic of seals used in Palestine: one sees here Egyptian influences (including the so-called sign of life), combined with motifs from north Mesopotamia. **50.** Side of the statue of Rameses II at Luxor, visible on p. 71, left. Each of the figures in the row underneath, depicted as Semites with their arms bound behind their backs and linked together by a halter around their necks, represents a region or city conquered in 'Asia'. One finds here well known names such as that of the kingdom of Mitanni (the second completely visible figure) which between 1460 and 1300 B.C. formed a buffer state between Assyria (fourth figure), the Hittites who had penetrated far into Syria (last in the row, not visible), and Egypt. In between are the names of regions and cities which have not yet all been identified. One can easily understand the importance of such lists for the study of the ancient political geography of Canaan. **53.** TOP: finds from Gibeon; *left*, the upper part of a wine jar with the funnel piece; the handles bear names; *right*, one of the many handles on which the name Gibeon occurs. FOOT: much cultural and historical information is derived from the discovery of numerous 'stelae', slabs of stone erected in honour of divinities or in commemoration, decorated in bas-relief and inscribed with texts. We give here three specimens: *Left:* a stele $4\frac{1}{2}$ ft. high, from the time of Tiglath-pileser III, found at *Arslân-Tash* west of Haran; the storm god Hadad stands on a young bull in a warlike attitude with a thunder bolt in each hand and a star symbol on his head; *upper right:* a stele of black basalt, 6 ft. high, found in the land of Moab, south of the Arnon near *el-Balu'a*, probably of the 12th or 11th century B.C. Between two gods in Egyptian dress stands a man praying, probably the king of Moab. The inscription on the top is scarcely visible and has not yet been deciphered. Equally indicative of strong Egyptian influence in Canaan is the small limestone stele below it, 11 in. high, dating from the 14th century B.C. and found in Beth-shan. Upper left can be seen the enthroned Mekal, the local baal of this city. **54.** Ostraca and seals. As writing material for notes and messages the ancient Israelites liked to use potsherds, which were provided in plenty by the household, rather than the expensive papyrus. Here are three examples of such potsherds ('ostraca'): *upper left*, a letter from Samaria, 8th century B.C., unfortunately broken off at the left-hand side. Two of the lines scratched upon it begin with the name Baruch, the third with the name Imna, which also occurs in the Bible. *Upper right*, one of the famous letters from Lachish. In 1953, in the gate building of the city, were found a number of potsherds of which unhappily only 18 still bore traces of lines written in ink in a flowing hand. Six of these presented a legible and coherent text. These letters were written to Yaôsh, apparently the Jewish governor of the district of Lachish in the anxious years of the Babylonian menace between 597 and 587. The writers, apparently officers serving in this area, employ exactly the same style as Baruch, the friend and secretary of Jeremiah, whom they undoubtedly all knew, if only by hearsay. Almost all the names of Judaeans mentioned in these letters occur also in the Bible. Our photograph shows the reverse of letter 3, giving the last five lines of what a certain Hoshaiah (cf. Jer 42 : 1) writes to Yaôsh and in which he mentions a letter from the royal official Tobiah addressed to Sallum, son of Jaddua, in the name of the prophet who says, 'Take heed.' *Centre right*, an ostracon of the 8th century found in the *Tell el-Qasîleh* slightly NE of Tel-Aviv, the site of a fortified Israelite trading city (it is not yet known which) during the time of the kings. The line reads 'Ophir gold [cf. Is 13 : 12] for Beth-horon . . .' Something else probably followed here. The letter and the three lines underneath mean 'thirty shekels'. Beth-horon, i.e. 'the house (temple) of the god Horon' is either the famous double city on the frontier between Israel and Judah or else a temple in the trading city mentioned. *Left centre*, five examples of seals from ancient Israel. They were usually made after the Egyptian model, in the shape of a scarab. This species of beetle lays its eggs in balls made from human or animal dung, which provides food for the larvae. From earliest times this insect was considered in Egypt as the symbol of the sun god who rolls across the sky the luminous ball from which all life emerges. The flat bottoms of the many scarab-shaped seals found in Egypt are decorated with all kinds of figures, formulas, and names. The upper two of our five illustrations show the surface and the impression of an Israelite scarab from Lachish; beneath the figure of a winged beetle stands the name of the owner, Ahimelech. Of the three illustrations beneath, the one on the left shows the impression from a scarab-like seal from Mizpah: above the fighting-cock is the name of the owner, 'Jaazaniah, the servant of the king' (see 2K 25 : 23). On the central impression the name Chaman can be read between the feet of a crowned sphinx (with the sign of life in front); below is a locust. *Right*, the bottom of a seal from the Transjordan; the cuneiform writing runs: 'Adoni-ner, servant of Amminadab' (king of the Ammonites *ca* 650 B.C.). At the foot of the page are four photographs of a rare scarab from the author's collection. It was found in Palestine and probably dates from the 16th century B.C. The figure stands in the attitude of a Pharaoh holding his enemies by the hair and on the point of striking. He is, however, obviously a Palestinian and what he is about to strike is Uraeus the serpent, on which he has also set his foot. This serpent is the symbol of Egyptian royal power. The various signs have not yet been fully explained. 55. TOP: vignette from the Leiden *Book of the Dead*. FOOT: papyrus with a classical work from the 3rd century B.C. Surrounding it, palettes of Egyptian scribes. 56. Statue of a scribe of the Old Kingdom from the Museum voor Oudheden in Leiden. He holds an unrolled papyrus on his knee and writes with his left hand. The sculptor did not devote much attention to the body; the head, on the other hand, is lovingly carved, 'a completely human portrait with delicate, well-formed features, pleasing both in full face and in profile'. 59. TOP: remains of a long table found in the large writing room in *Qumrân*, now in the Rockefeller Museum in Jerusalem. FOOT: part of another writing table. The hollows contained water in which it was probably customary to dip the fingers before writing the sacred name of Israel's god. The four consonants of this name, *Yhwh* (vowels were not written at this time), were represented in *Qumrân* either by the customary Hebrew letters, or the then old fashioned script of before the Exile (like that of the Lachish letters, see → 54, top right), or else with four dots. In later centuries, when reciting Biblical texts, the Jews were accustomed to replace the Name-of-four-letters (tetragram) by *Adonai*, which means 'the Lord'. When vowels were added to the sacred texts, the vowels of the word *Adonai* (a mute *e*, an *o*, and an *a*), which was to be pronounced, were added to the four sacred consonants. In the Middle Ages this fact was no longer understood and thus the four letters *Yhwh* were read with the vowels of Adonai, giving rise to the completely meaningless form of *Jehovah*. It is not entirely certain how the original sacred tetragram was pronounced. On good grounds scholars write and pronounce 'Yahweh' unless the name is avoided and replaced by 'the Lord' or 'the Eternal'. 60. TOP: one of the first and most famous finds at *Qumrân*. This scroll, 10¼ in. wide and 24 ft. long when unrolled, was found in a tall jar in cave No. 1 (see 140–141, foot). It contains the entire book of Isaiah as it is found in our Bible. On the second line of the completely visible column, after a white patch, begins Isaiah chapter 40: 'A voice cries: "In the wilderness prepare the way of the Lord" . . .' which words, slightly altered, are applied in the New Testament to John the Baptist, the voice in the wilderness. CENTRE: a particularly large fragment, 9 in. long and 4 in. broad, found in cave No. 4. It is part of a scroll which contained a commentary on Isaiah. The intact column reads: 'The meaning of the word concerns the end of time, at the destruction [?] of the earth by the sword and by famine; and it shall be in the time of the visitation of the earth: Woe to those who rise early in the morning, that they may run after strong drink . . . [Is 5 : 11–14]'. Then follows the commentary: 'These are the men of scorn who dwell in Jerusalem. They who have rejected the law of the Lord of Hosts, and have despised the words of the Holy One of Israel . . . [Is 5 : 24–25]'. After this follows again: 'This is the community of the men of scorn who are in Jerusalem . . .' One sees how the members of the Dead Sea sect considered their own situation and the circles of their enemies in

Jerusalem to have been already described in the old prophetic texts. FOOT: another fragment, seven-eighths of its true size, in which words of Isaiah 54 : 11–12 are applied to the community of the elect, cf. Revelation 21. RIGHT: reproduction in actual size of a phylactery or amulette. In Matthew 23 : 5 this is what is meant by the 'phylacteries' of the Pharisees. The specimen shown here dates from the time of Christ and was found in a cave on the *Wâdi Muraba'at*, 12½ miles south of *Qumrân*. Three of the prescribed texts are written on this strip in extremely small letters, Exodus 13 : 1–10, 13 : 11–16, and Deuteronomy 11 : 13–21. It was found in a small bag folded together with a smaller fragment on which is written the equally prescribed text of Deuteronomy 6 : 4–9: 'Hear O Israel . . .' (known as the *Shema*). **61.** TOP: the region around the city of *Harrân* has been under investigation since 1951. Our plate shows *Sultantepe*, 15½ miles north of Harrân. This tell has yielded, among other things, many hundreds of clay tablets from an Assyrian library. CENTRE: reconstruction sketch of the ziggurat of Ur, whose ground surface covers 205 ft. by 140 ft. FOOT: one of the sides of this massive structure; the man indicates the scale. **62.** A group of 'Asiatics' pay their respects to the Egyptian district governor Chnumhotep. From a wall painting in his tomb at *Beni-hasan*, 169 miles south of Cairo. The group of nomads, here cut into three, forms there a continuous whole. Behind the Egyptian official who presents the group to the much larger figure of Chnumhotep and upon whose papyrus one can read, among other things, the date (the 6th year of Sesostris II, i.e. roughly 1892 B.C.), follows another Egyptian. Then comes the leader of the group who makes a respectful gesture with his right hand. Between the horns of the ibex which he is offering one sees the crook with white stripes (cf. Gn 30 : 37) which on Egyptian pictures marks a Bedouin ruler. The hieroglyphs in front of his head give his title: 'ruler from a foreign land', those in front of his legs the name *Ibsha* (also read as Abisar). The inscription at the top means 'Arrival of black paint for the eyes, brought to him by 37 Asiatics'. The sign for the word 'Asiatics' is a bound man! The number 37 is unfortunately not visible on our reproduction. **65.** TOP: a Bedouin camp in the broad valley of the Brook Zered which divided the former regions of Moab and Edom. FOOT: the Jabbok, looking east. Note the two nomad tents. **66.** TOP: nomads in the desert east of Palestine near a pool recently created by the Jordan government. FOOT: an ancient oak near Hebron. **67.** TOP: view of *Tell Deir 'Alla* in the Jordan valley near the Jabbok, probably the Biblical Succoth, looking west. Behind the tell, the bed of the Jordan, behind that, the central mountain country. FOOT: aerial photograph of the plain in front of Shechem, taken from the north: 1 = Mount Gerizim; 2 = the massif of Mount Ebal; 3 = tell of ancient Shechem, to the left the small village of *Balâta*; 4 = unfinished church above Jacob's Well; 5 = the point from which photo → 68–69, foot, was taken; 6 = the road to the south, to Bethel and Jerusalem; 7 = the road to the north, to Tirzah, Tibhath, Beth-shan, etc.; 8 = the road to Samaria and the coastal plain; 9 = the road to the Jordan valley. **68.** TOP: aerial photograph, taken almost vertically, of the mountain pass between Mount Ebal and Mount Gerizim which can be seen left and right below. Between the small village of *Bal âta* and the refugee camp, top right, one can see a white building in a garden; this is the unfinished church above Jacob's Well. On the left-hand page can be seen the tell with the traces of the German excavations undertaken in 1913–1914 and continued from 1926–1934. Since 1956 (the photograph dates from 1953) an American expedition has been digging here every year. FOOT: a view through the pass from the east, from a point below 5 on p. 67, foot. Mount Gerizim, left, with the refugee camp in front of it, is completely visible; Mount Ebal, to the right, partly so. **70.** Rock formations on the shores of the Dead Sea. The projection upper right, 50 ft. high, resembles a fleeing woman and is called 'Lot's wife' by the Arabian inhabitants of this region who also usually call the Dead Sea *Bahr Lût*, the 'sea of Lot'. Below we see this figure in the distance, from a boat. **71.** Two statues of Rameses II at Luxor in front of the mighty hall with seven pairs of columns 52 ft. high, built by Amenophis III (1413–1377 B.C.) and visible in the centre of the aerial photograph → 22, foot. The side of the statue on the left is shown in close up on p. 50. **72.** Detail from a relief in the funeral chamber which Horemheb had built at Memphis while he was still a general under Akhenaton and Tutankhamon. Of the pieces scattered throughout many museums some are to be found in Leiden, including that showing the prisoners taken by the general in Asia. The detail shows two prisoners of whom the one on the left has the more pronounced Semitic features. In primitive handcuffs they are dragged along by two Egyptian soldiers, one of whom is hidden by the other. **75.** Details from a wall painting at Thebes, showing the making of bricks. **76.** TOP: en route for the heart of the Sinai peninsula. FOOT: the mountain mass traditionally thought to be the Biblical Sinai. The round peak on the left-hand side is the *Jebel Mûsa*, the mountain of Moses, 7467 ft. above sea-level, 2506 ft. above the monastery of St Catherine in the valley to the left. **77.** The monastery, developed from a fort which the emperor Justinian founded there in A.D. 530 to safeguard the neighbouring hermits. After flourishing for centuries (sometimes with as many as 400 monks) it decayed. The library contains countless old manuscripts. In 1950 an American expedition made microfilms of about 500,000 pages. **78.** TOP: the brook Arnon. FOOT: Mount Nebo. **81.** The enormous well in Gibeon; the spiral staircase descends beyond the bottom of the well as far as the spring water. **82.** TOP: The central hill country viewed from the east from a very great height. In the foreground is the edge of the Jordan valley (the white arrow points to the oval tell of ancient Jericho); behind lies the fantastic desert of Judaea. To the right can be seen the Jordan plain entering the central hill country. Here lay the way from Jericho to Ai and Bethel. In the distance are the white line of dunes and the sea coast, about 37 miles from Jericho. CENTRE: the small village of *el-Jîb* on the double hill on which Gibeon stood. The distant peak to the left, marked by a minaret, which rises 492 ft. above the plain and is visible for miles around, is probably the 'great high place' where Solomon offered sacrifice (1 K 3 : 4). Since the 5th century Samuel has been commemorated here, hence the name *Nebi Samwîl*, the prophet Samuel. FOOT: the city of Lachish according to a sketch made by the excavators. **83.** TOP: fully 130 ft. above the *Wâdi Waqqâs* in the foreground rises the tell of the same name. It is longitudinal in shape, about 1970 ft. long, averages 650 ft. across and is thus larger than that of Megiddo. Behind it, to the north, can be seen a plateau of roughly 3280 ft. by 2300 ft., with steep valleys behind and to the right. It is protected to the left by an artificial canal and an enormous earth wall, the base of which is 330 ft. thick in places. The English head of the Department of Antiquities, founded in 1920, identified this place with the ancient Hazor, made some investigations in 1928, and announced the plateau to be a fortified camp of the kind also found at Qatna and Carchemish. Since 1955 annual excavations have been made here under the leadership of Yigael Yadin, at both ends of the tell itself and at various places in the so-called camp. This proved indeed to be an extensive city destroyed shortly before 1200 B.C. Hazor is the only Palestinian city occurring in the archives of Mari (*ca* 1700 B.C.). It is found on the lists of the Pharaohs from Thothmes III onwards and is mentioned as a fortified city in the Amarna archives. Thanks in part to its excellent position on the great highway from Damascus and Mesopotamia to Egypt it was, as Joshua says (11 : 10), the principal royal city of the region. FOOT: the excavation of the eastern part of the tell in 1957; the building with the 6½ ft. high pillars dates from the time of Ahab. Below, left, are the foundations of the gate building dating from the time of Solomon, exactly resembling that of Megiddo (cf. 1 K 9 : 15). **84.** TOP: view from the overgrown ruins of Megiddo looking northeast. Across the plain of Jezreel can be seen Mount Tabor to the right and to the left of it the hills of Lower Galilee. FOOT: the top of Mount Tabor from an aeroplane (see → 27 for a view from the tower of the Latin basilica on the summit right across the Greek monastery). Below the two buildings are the ruins of earlier churches and houses. **87.** A Philistine and a Semite, detail from a relief which shows bound prisoners being brought before Rameses III. From his temple at Thebes. **88.** TOP: the village of *Jebaʿ*, the Biblical Geba, 6 miles NNW of old Jerusalem. The shadow to the upper right is that of the deep pass on the other side of which lies the village of *Mukhmâs*, the Biblical Michmash. FOOT: entrance to the pass between Geba and Michmash, the scene of Jonathan's heroic deed (see 1 S 14 : 4–5). **89.** TOP: bronze idols from Canaan; these idols often still bear traces of gold leaf. FOOT: the plain of Jezreel; *left*, the *Jebel Dahi*, probably identical with the hill of Moreh of Judges 7 : 1; *right*, the mountain range of Gilboa; between the two the plain slopes down to the Jordan. There lies Beth-shan. The Transjordan highland can just be seen in the distance. The numbers indicate the following Biblical places: 1 = En-dor;

2 = Nain; 3 = Shunem; 4 = Jezreel. **90**. TOP: *left*, a throne from the tomb of Tutankh amon. This Pharaoh, who abandoned the 'heresy' of his predecessor and father-in-law Akhenaton and returned to Thebes, was buried after his short reign (1358-1349 B.C.) with magnificent treasures by the grateful priests in the Valley of the Kings The throne, made of precious woods and inset with ivory and gold, has a footstool on which the nine traditional enemies of Egypt are depicted – in this connection we must remember that to the Egyptians anything depicted was considered in a certain sense to be really present. *Right*, Thothmes III sitting at the right hand of the supreme god of Thebes, Amon, whose statue was originally larger than that of the Pharaoh. It fell a victim, however, to Akhenaton's religious fervour and was so badly damaged that the later restoration, in which the god was made smaller, could not stand the test of time. FOOT: the footstool of the throne; the text in the middle begins at the top and reads: 'All lands, every foreign land, the chiefs of the whole of Retenu as one under our two sandals equal [under] Re for ever'. Retenu is an Egyptian name for the coastal region of Syria and Palestine; Re is the sun god. **95**. TOP: music and dance in ancient Egypt; relief from an unfinished temple of Hatshepsut at Karnak. FOOT: relief from the mortuary chapel of Patenemheb (*ca* 1350 B.C.) now in Leiden; behind the priest, who is performing the funeral sacrifice (he is wearing an animal skin) sit four musicians with their instruments – a harp, a lute, and two flutes. The harpist, also shown on the wrapper of this book, 'far surpasses the others in beauty. What splendour upon a surface of a few square centimetres! The sunken features, the desolate pose, the dead eyes, it is the blind man as we have all seen him in daily life' (Guide to the Museum). Also well known is the hieroglyphic text above the scene in which the harpist sings of the transitoriness of all famous men and of their tombs and the inevitability of death: 'No-one returns from thence to tell us what a man needs there and to calm our fears until we too arrive where they have gone before. Follow your desire as long as you live; lay myrrh upon your head and clothe yourself in fine linen. Increase your possessions and do not give way to dejection. Do what you will upon earth and do not torment your heart before the day of tears arrives...' (cf. Ecclesiastes). **96**. TOP: view northwards through the Kidron valley. *Right*, against the Mount of Offence, on the slope which in the time of the Kings contained many rock tombs, is the modern village of *Silwân* (the name reminds us of Siloam). In the background is the high temple terrace. FOOT: photograph taken in almost the same direction but from the air. **97**. TOP: aerial photograph of Jerusalem. The numbers (those in *italic* type also occur on the photograph below) are: *1* = Kidron valley; *2* = Tyropoeon valley; *3* = Spring Gihon; *4* = the Garden of Gethsemane (for *5* see description of next photograph); *6* = the ancient road to Jericho across the slopes of the Mount of Olives; *7* = Dominus Flevit; 13 = the church above Calvary and the Holy Sepulchre; 14 = the three towers of Herod's palace; 15 = Church of the Cenacle (traditional site of the Last Supper and the miracle on Whit Sunday). FOOT: aerial photograph of Jerusalem: 5 = the modern asphalt road to Jericho which runs through Bethany; 8 = the site of Bethphage; 9 = mosque on the traditional scene of the Ascension; 10 = German hospital on the site of Nob; 11 = site of the village of Bahurim (2 S 16 : 5); 12 = Anathoth. **98**. TOP: bronze statue of a calf from Hazor. FOOT: objects used in religious ceremonies; *left*, model of a laver on a stand, 15½ in. high, dating from the 12th century B.C., found in a tomb in Cyprus. The ornamentation includes winged sphinxes and birds at the corners. *Right*, an altar from Megiddo 21½ in. high, from a slightly later period; note the 'horn' at each corner. **101**. Examples of carved ivory. This art flourished in Syria in the time of Israel's kings. To decorate wooden panels, chairs, couches, etc., all kinds of figures, inspired by motifs from Egypt, Mesopotamia, and the Greek islands, were carved from small ivory tablets. The pieces shown here come from Hazael's palace in Damascus (found, however, as war booty of the Assyrians of *Arslân-Tash*), from Megiddo, and from the palace of Ahab at Samaria (cf. for example Am 3 : 15, 6 : 4). One can imagine this kind of carving when reading descriptions of the decoration of Solomon's temple: 'carved figures of cherubim, and palm trees and open flowers' (1 K 6 : 29). **102**. TOP: reconstruction sketch of the temple of Solomon from data supplied by G. Wright and W. F. Albright. The two pillars, called Joachim and Boaz (probably after the first words of their inscriptions) were made entirely of bronze and were

over 32 ft. high. FOOT: reconstruction drawing of one of the gates of Megiddo, fortified by Solomon. **103.** TOP: Canaanite temple found in the most northern part of Hazor. Of the three rooms which correspond with the entrance hall, the main hall, and the rear hall (the Holy of Holies) of Solomon's temple, we see here the rear hall. The floor is strewn with religious objects and surrounded by a series of skilfully made long basalt tiles (a Hittite method of construction) on which wooden beams evidently lay to strengthen the brick wall above. The central and entrance halls are visible in the background. In front of the entrance were found two round basalt pillar bases. The temple, 82 ft. long and 56 ft. wide and, judging from traces of fire, suddenly and completely destroyed around the year 1200 B.C., had thus two pillars before the entrance, exactly like the temple of Solomon. FOOT: some objects used in the religious services. In front, an overturned incense altar of basalt, 4½ ft. high and 2 ft. broad. The star within a circle is the emblem of the Canaanite sun god. Also visible are two basalt slabs with rectangular hollows, obviously for the libations with the liquids (oil or wine) which were stored in the magnificent jars. **104.** Canaanite ruler; detail from an ivory tablet (bottom picture), 10 in. long, found at Megiddo. Judging from the holes (see bottom photograph) it was mounted on some object (a sheath?). The king, drinking from a bowl and reaching with his other hand for a lotus flower, sits upon a throne supported by two winged animals with human heads, the cherubim, perhaps an illustration of the cherubim on which the divine ruler of Israel was invisibly enthroned in the Holy of Holies. The woman before him who is handing him the lotus, appears to be offering a piece of her shawl as a napkin. On the rather indistinct plate below, a figure can be seen behind her playing a nine-stringed lyre (as David did before Saul); then follow naked prisoners walking bound before an officer riding in a war chariot with two horses in front of it and the winged sun floating above. **105.** TOP: The city of Tirzah at the head of the valley which runs in a southeasterly direction towards the valley of the Jordan (visible on → 11, left). FOOT: the isolated hill on which King Omri built his new capital of Samaria; it later bore Herod's splendid city, Sebaste, whose name is perpetuated in the modest village of *Sebastiyeh*. **106.** TOP: entrance to the water tunnel of Gibeon directly behind the city wall, whose foundations can be seen. FOOT: two water tunnels; *left*, that of Gibeon, *right*, that of Jerusalem, built under King Hezekiah (2 K 20 : 20). Its course (560 yds.) is given on Map 4. It carried the water from the Spring Gihon to a pool in a later part of the city which lay well within the walls. **107.** TOP: the walls of the city which lay on the *Tell en-Nasbeh*, 8 miles north of Jerusalem, after a sketch made by the excavators who think that the important city of Mizpah may well lie here. FOOT: sketch of a water tunnel: behind the city wall (here partly omitted) begins the tunnel which leads to the space in which the water bubbles up out of the ground (near 2); the low entry from outside could be closed with a stone in such a way that no enemy could force it (above 1). For the excess water a narrow exit was made elsewhere. **108.** Detail from a four-sided commemorative stele of Shalmaneser III from his palace at Calah (*Nimrûd*) now in the British Museum. According to the text (magnificently engraved cuneiform writing), it represents the offering of 'the tribute of Jehu, son of Omri'. He was, however, not a son but a usurper of the throne of this great ruler of Israel. **111.** Relief, fully 37 ft. high, from the palace of Ashurbanipal at Nineveh, now in the British Museum. According to the inscription at the top (not visible) the destruction of the royal city of Hamanu in Elam is depicted here. **112.** TOP: reconstruction drawing by the excavators of Dur-Sharrukîn, the citadel built by Sargon II and intended as the court capital. It was abandoned by his son Sennacherib in favour of Nineveh and was therefore rediscovered comparatively intact. Note the ziggurat. FOOT: King Ashurbanipal hunting wild asses; relief (21 in. high) from Nineveh, now in the British Museum. **113.** TOP: the storming of a city in the time of Tiglath-pileser III, now in the British Museum. FOOT: deportation of the inhabitants of the city of Astartu (according to the inscription), probably the Biblical Ashtaroth, east of the Sea of Galilee. From the palace at Calah. **114.** Ashurbanipal in his state chariot; detail from a relief from Nineveh, now in the Louvre. To Isaiah the Assyrian world ruler is destructive, proud, and cruel, the opposite of the true ruler Yahweh and his Anointed. **119.** The western spur of the Carmel range, seen from the beach of the bay of Acco. At the foot lies Haifa, founded from Tyre in the 4th century B.C. Only in recent times has it developed into one of the most important cities of Palestine. **120.** TOP: the village of '*Anâta* seen from the hill upon which lie the ruins of Jeremiah's Anathoth. FOOT: the spring of Parah 3 miles east northeast of Anathoth. **121.** TOP: a man on a flat threshing board which is drawn by two muzzled oxen. FOOT: winnowers. **122.** Detail of → 111. **125.** The Babylon of Nebuchadnezzar after a drawing by E. Unger based on the excavations. In the foreground is the bridge over the Euphrates, behind, the temple complex with the 'tower of Babel' (ground surface 295 sq. ft.) the famous processional route leads from here through the city. **126.** TOP: Persepolis, the magnificent court capital of Darius (521–485 B.C.) and Xerxes (485–464) where they received the yearly gifts of the tributary peoples and which was completely destroyed by Alexander the Great. Here, from Babylonian, Assyrian, Greek, and Egyptian motifs, the Persians developed their own style of architecture. FOOT: one of the delegations with gifts, detail from the reliefs which were exposed on the front of the palace terrace during the investigations of 1931–1934. They are rouglhy 330 ft. in length. **127.** TOP: coin from Judah, struck during the Persian domination but following the Attic model and bearing the owl of Athenc. The three letters to the right are read as *J. H. D.*, the Aramaic form (Jehud) of the name Judah which occurs in the books of Ezra and Daniel. FOOT. silver spoon, 9 in. long, dated between 450 and 330 B.C., found in a tomb on the southern coastal plain. Spoons with handles consisting of a female body were very widespread in ancient Egypt; the elaboration of this idea, however, is here purely Syrian, as can be seen from the face of the woman, the two bulls' heads near the ring and the lotus motif between her hands. **128.** TOP: Alexander the Great shown as a god with the ram's horns, on a tetradrachm of *ca* 295 B.C. FOOT: representatives of the two dynasties which fought for the possession of Palestine: *left*, Ptolemy I (305–283), and *right*, Antiochus the Great (223–187). **131.** TOP: a folded and sealed contract from Elephantine on which can be read: *spr bt zî ktb*, 'letter concerning a house, written by . . .' Below, the first lines of such a contract. FOOT: the Nile near Assuân, which is visible right, in the background. Elephantine is not the island in the foreground but the larger one behind it; on the photograph it is barely distinguishable from the city. Right, in the background, is the first cataract (counting from Cairo), where the Nile has to force its way through enormous blocks of granite. Here there are no fertile strips. **132.** TOP: *left*, Alexandrian coin from the time of Commodus (A.D. 161–192), with the famous lighthouse on the island of Pharos, and a sailing ship. *Right*, a reconstruction drawing of the 460 ft. high construction which was built under Ptolemy II Philadelphus (283–246 B.C.) and was considered one of the wonders of the world. FOOT: for the Egyptian god Horus whom the Ptolemies equated with the Greek Apollo, they built (in many stages, beginning in 237 B.C.) the magnificent temple at Edfu (62½ miles south of Luxor) which was then called Apollinopolis. Almost completely buried in Nile silt until the end of last century, this temple is considered one of the best preserved constructions of ancient times. Erected according to the classical Egyptian model, the details bear evidence of the strong influence of Greek culture. **133.** LEFTS: five coins; the upper specimen shows Antiochus IV Epiphanes (175–163 B.C.), who after his victory over Ptolemy VI in 169 began to call himself 'Theos Epiphanes', 'god made manifest in the flesh', and later added the title of Nikephoros, by which he in fact identified himself with Zeus. On the next coin he has had himself depicted with the wreath of victory and the beard of Zeus. The third coin shows Ptolemy III Euergetes, the deified 'benefacor'; of his subjects, with the aureole of the sun god and the trident of Poseidon. Finally, the obverse and reverse of a Jewish coin of Alexander Jannaeus (Jannai was a childish form of Jonathan); the text in archaic letters reads: 'Jonathan high priest and the community of the Jews'. On other coins of his one reads on one side 'Jonathan the king' in Hebrew, and on the other 'of King Alexander' in Greek, RIGHT: Cleopatra; relief from ther well-peserved Ptolemaic-Roman temple at Denderah (31 miles north of Luxor), dedicatede ft the goddess Hathor who was identified with Aphrodite. **134.** Roman soldiers witohtsandards crossing a ship bridge; detail from the column of Trajan in Rome. **137.** Corner of the great temple square at Palmyra (see → 139, foot), showing that the influence of Greek taste reached far into the Syrian desert. Left, the monumental entrance gate to thee city beyond it, an Arabian fort. **138.** TOP: three tomb monuments at the entrance to the narrow cleft in the rocks which gives access to Petra. They were made by cutting away the surrounding rock. The monument on the left (note the small figure) appears to be an imitation of an altar. FOOT: one of the countless tombs hewn out of the rose-red rock walls surrounding the city; *right*, an aerial photograph of the west side of Petra; the small rock in the centre bore the acropolis of this immensely wealthy trading city which extended into the valley on the left and knew its greatest period of prosperity during the first century of our era (King Aretas IV even ruled Damascus, see 2 Co 11 : 32). The enormous, steep rock which can be seen above the acropolis and whose top lies 66½ ft. higher than the city, is considered to be the site of the Edomite capital of Sela (the name means 'rock' as does Petra) which was conquered by Amaziah (2 K 14 : 7, 2 Ch 25 : 12). **139.** TOP: the famous temple complex of Ba'albek, dedicated to the Baal of the Beqa', who, after the time of Alexander, was identified with Helios the sun god and venerated by the Romans as Jupiter Heliopolitanus. In his honour they built in the 2nd century A.D. the structure which has suffered much from attacks and earthquakes and in which a Christian church and an Arabian fort were built. On the plate can be seen, to the right, one of the restored exedrae in the arcade which surrounded the great forecourt (394 x 328 ft.); left, behind the gully which contained the foundations of the church which has now been pulled down, can be seen an altar and then the mighty entrance stairway to the temple of Jupiter, 24 ft. higher. Of its 54 pillars, 66 ft. high and 7 ft. in diameter, only six remain. FOOT: an aerial photograph of Palmyra, the trading city in the desert which flourished in the 2nd century A.D., replacing Petra in importance. The temple in the foreground (the sides are 820 ft. long; in 1935 a whole village was removed from it!) was begun when Jesus was a boy. Above the sanctuary in the centre can be seen the corner which is shown in close up on → 137; behind it is the monumental gate to the central arcade. **140–141.** TOP: the rock wall and the plateau of *Qumrân* seen from near the shore of the Dead Sea. FOOT: the position of cave No. 1. **142.** TOP: the plateau of *Qumrân* seen from the high rock wall; in the background is the northern part of the Dead Sea. FOOT: an aerial view of the plateau. **143.** An aerial photograph in a southerly direction; the rectangular ruin is clearly visible in the foreground; behind slopes the fantastic wâdi wall which, together with the steep mountain wall to the right, forms the background of the next photograph. *Upper right*, the fantastic relief of the desert of Judaea. **144.** The spur in which cave No. 4 is situated. **147.** TOP: the ruin on the plateau; to the right is the spur from which the preceding photograph was taken, looking towards cave No. 4. FOOT: the examination of a cave; the soil is carefully scraped away and then carried outside in baskets. **148.** TOP: the refectory of the fraternity. FOOT: the steps of one of the many cisterns; the left half has subsided as the result of an earthquake. **149.** TOP: most of the documents were found in small fragments; cave 4 alone yielded thousands, from hundreds of different manuscripts. FOOT: with infinite patience an international team of scholars in the Rockefeller Museum sorts and studies the fragments. A small selection carefully held together between glass plates, is spread out on the tables. **150.** Young shepherd wearing a head-cloth, followed by his sheep. **155.** The village of *Kafr Kenna*. **156.** TOP: Bethlehem. FOOT: shepherds in the so-called 'field of the shepherds' near Bethlehem, which can just be seen in the background. **157.** TOP: the only remaining part of Herod's temple in Samaria, built in honour of Augustus; the entrance stairway. FOOT: the tomb of Abraham at Hebron with the magnificent ring wall of Herod which can be seen in close-up on the right. **158.** TOP: village in Galilee. FOOT: present-day Nazareth; in the background can be seen the plain of Jezreel whose name was corrupted in Christian times to Esdraelon. **161.** TOP: one of the many bends of the Jordan. FOOT: the Jordan near Jericho; in the background are the fantastic marl hills which flank the river bed (see → 41, → 11). **162.** Part of the wilderness of Judaea; in the foreground are the enclosures of stones in which the shepherds gather their sheep at night; the dark patches are cultivated land. Above the centre is the cone-shaped ruin of the Herodium, the fortress which Herod built and destined to be his tomb. Above it are the little houses of the village of *Beit Sahûr* and to the left is Bethlehem. **163.** TOP: a man draws water from a cistern for a woman who will carry the filled jars on her head back to her tent. FOOT: a farmer ploughing his land, a thin layer of soil strewn with stones, on a foundation of rock. **164–165.** Tiberias on the

Sea of Galilee; the inhabitants of the other shore had more contact with those on this side than with the people of the barely accessible highland behind them. **166.** TOP: the temple square in Jerusalem. FOOT: the Kidron valley with the corner of the temple square which is partly visible on the preceding photograph. The sepulchral monument in the centre probably existed in the time of Christ, the Jewish tombs are of a much later date. **167.** LEFT: perfume jars and lamps from a tomb on the Mount of Olives dating from the time of Christ. At the bottom of the page is an inscription on an ossuarium found there; it reads: 'Martha and Mary'. RIGHT: top, a street in Jerusalem; *foot*, a street which descends from the upper town to the old hill of Zion, a street where Jesus may have walked. **168.** TOP: the usual disposition of the Jewish graves around Jerusalem in the time of Herod; an open passage (1) was hewn in the slope of a hill, usually with a few steps in order to attain the required depth more quickly. Behind a very low opening, which could be sealed by rolling a stone in front of it, a room was dug out (2) with benches against the walls (2a) and then a second room (3) with one or more niches in the walls in which the dead were placed (3a). The floor of the niche often sloped slightly so that the fluid produced by decomposition could run off into a hole. After a time only the skeleton remained, and it was collected when the niche was required for another body and buried either in a small opening in the floor or in a small chest (ossuarium). FOOT: the entrance to a tomb near Jerusalem, with a stone. **171.** TOP: the arrival of a Roman trading ship, probably in the port of Ostia; the captain offers sacrifice on the rear deck in thanksgiving for a safe return. To the right of the ship stands Neptune; other statues stand in various places in the harbour. On the base of one of them is depicted a chariot drawn by four elephants; the rider is perhaps the emperor Claudius, the founder of the harbour. This relief contains many interesting details; the structure of the ship, the rigging, the sails, the sloops, etc. St Paul travelled in ships like these. Relief, 3rd century A.D., *Museo Torlonia, Rome.* FOOT: Roman milestone beside an ancient highway that leads over the fertile highland from Dibon to Medeba *(Madaba),* visible in the distance. **172.** In the footsteps of St Paul. TOP LEFT: entry gate to the 'Street called Straight' in Damascus, the *Cardo maximus* which formed the main street in all Graeco-Roman towns. The little gate is really the side gate of the monumental entry of which the main arch was to the left. TOP RIGHT: the Lechaion way in Corinth, often travelled by St Paul. FOOT: Antioch on the Orontes; from the ruins of the citadel modern Antakya can be seen. Apart from a few ruins it retains no trace of the glittering capital of the Seleucids but the name. Antioch was once one of the most important centres for the propagation of the Christian message. **173.** The Cilician Gates, one of the passes through the Taurus mountains, which St Paul frequently crossed with great danger. **174.** TOP LEFT: the Artemis of the Ephesians, a marble statue with bronze head, hands, and feet. *Museo dei Conservatori, Rome.* TOP RIGHT: altar dedicated to an unknown god on the Palatine in Rome. FOOT: detail from a relief on the inner side of the triumphal arch of Titus on the Forum in Rome. Romans wearing wreaths bear in triumph the massive seven-branched candlestick from the destroyed temple of Jerusalem.

ACKNOWLEDGMENTS

Roman numerals indicate the position of photographs on the page, starting at the top and proceeding from left to right down the page.

Agence Rapho, Paris 147 (ii), 148 (i); Alinari, Florence 128 (ii, iii); 134, 171 (i), 174; Allegro, Manchester 59 (i, ii), 149 (i); Arab Legion Air Force, 'Ammân 35 (i), 67 (ii), 68–69 (i), 88 (i), 142 (ii), 143, 162; Archives Photographiques, Paris 89 (i, *centre and right*), 133 (ii); British Museum, London 61 (iii), 108; Brown, E.E. 97 (ii); Consulate of Israel, Amsterdam 28 (ii): Creten, Canon J., Louvain 76 (i); Department of Antiquities, 'Ammân 34 (i), 54 *(centre, fifth seal),* 60 *(right);* Department of Antiquities, Israel 54 *(centre, right);* Dunand, Maurice, Beirut 30; École Biblique et Archéologique Française, Jerusalem 70, 76 (ii), 168 (ii); Elia Photo Service, Jerusalem 97 (i); Elsevier, N. V. Uitgeversmaatschappij, Amsterdam 71, 121 (i), 126, 132 (ii), 163 (i), 172 (ii); Eyckeler, J., Druten 157 (i); Galloway, E., New York 161 (ii); Giegel, Zurich, 150, 155; Giraudon, Paris 49 (*third row, right*); Grollenberg Collection 11, 24; Grollenberg, L., O.P. 13 (ii), 19, 20–21, 23, 27, 29, 33 (ii), 34 (ii), 35 (ii), 36, 39 (*left row, bottom row*, and *vessels 2, 4, 5, 6*), 40 (i), 41 (i), 42, 48, 49 (*top*), 50, 54 (*bottom row*), 65 (ii), 67 (i), 78 (i), 82 (ii), 84 (i), 95 (i), 96 (i), 105 (i), 120, 121 (ii), 131 (iii), 132 (iii), 137, 138 (iii), 139 (i), 140–141, 142 (i), 144, 147 (i), 148 (ii), 157 (ii), 158 (ii), 161 (i), 167 (ii), 171 (ii), 172 (i, iii); Hendrikse, P. (for data supplied to the author) 107 (ii), 168 (i); *Illustrated London News*, London 49 (*bottom row*), 89 (i, *left figure*), 90 (i, iii); Institut Français d'Archéologie, Beirut 12 (i), 13 (i), 17, 18, 33 (i), 139 (ii); Israel Information Service, New York 89 (ii), 164–165; Keren Hayesod, Jerusalem 158 (i); Koninklijk Kabinet van Munten en Penningen en gesneden Stenen, The Hague 49 (*third row, left*), 128 (i), 132 (i), 133 (*coins*); Laxague, H.D., O.P., Oullins 78 (ii), 138 (i); Lelong, P., Paris 167 (iii); Lloyd, Dr Seton, Ankara 61 (i); Louvre, Musée du, Paris 47, 53 (iii, *left*), 113 (ii), 114; Maliepaard, Ir. C. H. J., The Hague 66 (i); Mansell Collection, London 111, 112 (ii), 113 (i), 122; Matson Photo Service, Los Angeles 77, 96 (ii), 119, 156; Oriental Institute, Chicago 87; Ploeg, Dr J. van der, O.P. 166 (ii); Pennarts and Glissenaar, Montfoort 65 (i), 88 (ii), 105 (ii); Poll, W. van de, Amsterdam 12 (ii), 34 (iii), 68–69 (ii), Popper, Paul, London 84 (i), 166 (i), 173; Pritchard, J. B., Berkeley, California 53 (i, ii), 81, 106 (i, ii); Rockefeller Museum, Jerusalem 39 (*pottery vessels 1 and 3*), 41 (ii, iii, iv), 49 (*second row*), 53 (iii, *right*), 54 (*top row and centre left, 4 seals*), 60 (*centre and foot*), 98 (iii), 101 (*top and foot*), 104 (ii), 106 (iii), 127 (*spoon*), 138 (ii), 149 ii); Rijksmuseum voor Oudheden, Leiden 40 (ii), 55 (i, ii *palettes*), 56, 72, 95 (ii); Schweig, Jerusalem 28 (i); Spaarnestad, Messrs, Haarlem 22; Stroete, P. G. te, Nijmegen 157 (iii), 163 (ii); *The Times*, London 82 (i); Yadin, Y., Jerusalem 83, 98 (i), 103.

ILLUSTRATIONS FROM BOOKS

60 (i), 102 (i): *The Biblical Archaeologist*, New Haven, U.S.A.; 131 (ii): Kraeling, E. G., *The Brooklyn Museum Aramaic Papyri*, New Haven, U.S.A., 1953; 150, 155: Bruin, P. and Giegel, P., *Hier hat Gott Gelebt*, Zürich; 90 (ii): Legrain, *Status et Statuettes;* 112 (i): Loud, G. and Altman, C. B., *Khorsabad*, Part II, Chicago, 1938; 107 (i): McCown, *Tell en-Nasbe;* 102 (ii): *The Megiddo Expedition, Megiddo II;* 127 (*coin*): Reigenberg, A., *Ancient Jewish Coins*, Jerusalem, 1947; 55 (iii): W. Schubart, *Papyri Graeci Berolineuses;* 101 (*centre*): Thureau-Dangin, F., Barrois, A., Dossing, G., and Dunand, M., *Arslân-Tash*, Paris, 1932; 82 (iii): Torczyner, H., Harding, L. and others, *Lachish I – The Lachish Letters*, London, 1938; 125: Unger, E., *Babylon*, Leipzig, 1931; 62, 75: Vigouroux, F., *Dictionnaire de la Bible*, Paris 1895–1912; 14: Wreszinski, *Atlas zur altägyptischen Kulturgeschichte*, Leipzig, 1923.

The author's grateful thanks are due to P. B. Bagatti, O. F. M. (for 41ʋ and 167 *left and foot*) and P. M. E. Boismard (both of Jerusalem), R. J. Demarée (The Hague), Madame Desroches-Noblecourt (Paris), Dr R. Frankena (Leiden), J. van der Ploeg, O.P., P. Jean-Roger A. A. (Jerusalem), Dr A. A. Kampman (Leiden), J. B. Pritchard (Berkeley, U.S.A.), Dr W. D. van Wijngaarden (Leiden) and Y. Yadin (Jerusalem) for their kind co-operation in obtaining and interpreting some of the photographs.

187

INDEX

In this index references are given to the pages of the book and to the maps. Pages on which photographs occur are in *italic* type. A star indicates that further information will be found in the Notes on the Plates (pp. 175–186). The letters EP denote the map on the front end-paper.

The following abbreviations are used when referring to plates, to indicate the position of the photograph on the page: t = top; f = foot; c = centre; l = left; r = right.

BIBLICAL REFERENCES

GENESIS (Gn)		**JUDGES (Jg)**	
I	57, 124	I : 27–35	80
10	51	2 : 6–3 : 4	86
10 : 6	15	5	86
10 : 18	51	5 : 19	52
11 : 3	31	10 : 6–16	86
12–50	63f.		
14 : 18–24	94	**2 SAMUEL (2 S)**	
15 : 6	64	2 : 13	52
17	64, 124	5 : 8	92
18, 19	64	7	92
19 : 30–38	64	8	92
22 : 20–24	86	9–20	92
25 : 13–16	86	12 : 28	92
25 : 22–26	63	16 : 5	97f★
30 : 37	62★	20 : 1	99

EXODUS (Ex)		**1 KINGS (1 K)**	
12 : 38	74	1–2	92
13 : 1–16	60 r★	3 : 4	82 c★
25–31	124	4 : 7–20	94
35–40	124	5 : 18	31
		6 : 29	101★
NUMBERS (Num)		9 : 15	83f★
11 : 4	74	11	99
13 : 16	85	12 : 16	99
		13–14	100

DEUTERONOMY (Dt)		**2 KINGS (2 K)**	
6 : 4–9	60 r★	14 : 7	138 f★
11 : 13–21	60 r★	17	100
11 : 14	26	20 : 20	106 f★
25 : 4	118	25 : 14	123
26 : 5–10	63	25 : 23	54★
34 : 1–8	57		

JOSHUA (Jos)		**1 CHRONICLES (1 Ch)**	
3 : 16	11★	11 : 6	92
11 : 10	83 t★		
13–21	51	**2 CHRONICLES (2 Ch)**	
13 : 27	51	25 : 12	138 f★
15	80		
17 : 11–13	80	**EZRA**	
21 : 45	80	1 : 7	123
23 : 15	80		
24	80	**PSALMS (Ps)**	
		2 : 7	91

89	92		
110 : 1	91		
132	92		
PROVERBS (Pr)			
1–9	124		
10–22	94, 124		
25–29	94, 124		
ISAIAH (Is)			
5 : 11–14	60 c★		
5 : 24–25	60 c★		
5 : 25–29	118		
7 : 17	99		
10 : 9	Map 6		
10 : 28–34	118		
13 : 12	54★		
21 : 10	118		
24–27	124		
28 : 21	92		
30, 31	135		
40–55	117		
40 : 1	60 t★		
54 : 11–12	60f★		
JEREMIAH (Jer)			
13 : 4–7	118		
30 : 18	32		
39 : 3	48 c★		
42 : 1	54★		
EZEKIEL (Ezk)			
27 : 9	31		
29 : 10	124		
30 : 6	124		
34 : 16	151		
38–39	124		
DANIEL (Dn)			
11 : 20	135		
11 : 30	135		
AMOS			
3 : 15	101★		
6 : 4	101★		

MACCABEES (2 Mac)		3 : 1	153	9	169
: 7ff.	135	7 : 11	Map 8	9–11	Map 8
MATTHEW (Mt)		19 : 12, 14	153	9 : 32	Map 8
2 : 22	153	24 : 13	Map 8	9 : 35	Map 8
2 : 23	Map 8	JOHN (Jn)		10	169, Map 8
4 : 13	Map 8	1 : 28	159	13	169
16 : 13	Map 8	2 : 1	27 *t*★, Map 8	17 : 23	170
23 : 5	60 *r*★	3 : 23	159, Map 8	19 : 27	170
27 : 57	Map 8	4	Map 8	21 : 7	Map 8
MARK (Mk)		11 : 54	Map 8	22	169
6 : 14–29	Map 8	ACTS (Ac)		23 : 31	Map 8
LUKE (Lk)		2–4	169	26	169
2 : 49	159	8 : 26	Map 8	2 CORINTHIANS (2 Co)	
		8 : 40	Map 8	11 : 32	138 *f*★

PERSONS, PLACES, AND THINGS

A

Abel-beth-maacah   Map 5
Abel-keramim   Map 3
Abel-meholah   Maps 3, 5
Abel-shittim   Map 3
Abijam   116
Abila   Map 8
Abisar   62★
Abraham 63, 151, *157 f*★, Map 2
Accad   EP
Accadians   45
Acco 26, 130, *119*★, Maps 1, 2, 3, 5
Achaia   Map 9
Achmetha   EP
Achshaph   Map 3
Actium   136
Acts   152, 169
Adad-nirari III   110, 116
Adam (man)   94
Adam (place)   *11*★, Map 3
Admah   Map 2
Adonai   59★
Adoni-ner   54★
Adoraim   Map 5
Adramyttium   Map 9
Adullam   Maps 3, 5
Aenon   159
Agrippa I   152, 153
Agrippa II   152, 153
Ahab, King 100, 109, 115 116, *83 f*★, *101*★
Ahaz   116
Ahaziah   116
Ahijah   99, 116
Ai   79, 85, Map 3

Aiath   118
Aijalon   Maps 3, 5
Akeldama   Map 4
Akhenaton   73, *90 t*★
'Aqir   52
Alalakh   Map 2
Albinus   152
Aleppo   Maps 2, EP
Alexander the Great   129, *17 f*★, *18 f*★, *126 t*△, *128 t*, Map 6
Alexander Jannaeus   135, 133★
Alexandria   129, *132 t*, Maps 7, EP
Alexandrium   Map 8
Almon   118
Alphabet   32, 51
Altar   *98 fr*★
Amanus   Map 2
Amarna archives   83★
Amaziah   116, *138 f*★
Ambibulus, Marcus, 152
Amenophis III   51, *71*★
Amenophis IV   44, 51, 73
Amminadab   54★
'Ammân   Map 1
Ammon   64, 109, Maps 3, 5, 6
Ammon, Oasis of   Map 7
Ammonites   86
Amon   91
Amon (king of Judah) 116
Amos   116, 117, 118
Amphipolis   Map 9
Amrît   *40 t*★
Amygdalon   Map 4
Anab   Map 3

'Anâta   118, *120t*
Anathoth   118, *97 f*, *120t*
Ancyra (*Ankara*)   Maps 7, EP
Andrew   160
Annius Rufus   152
Antakya   *172 f*★
Antigonus   136
Anti-Lebanon   10, Map 2
Antioch 129, 151, *172 f*★, Maps 9, EP
Antioch (in Pisidia) Map 9
Antiochus III   130, 135, *128 f*★
Antiochus IV   130, 135, 133★
Antipater   136
Antipatris   Map 8
Antonia   Map 4
Apamea   129
Aphek, later Antipatris   Maps 3, 5
Aphek (in Asher)   Map 3
Aphek (in Transjordan)   Map 5
Aphrodite   *133 r*★
Apollo   *132 f*★
'Aqaba   9
Arabah   9, *28 f*
Arad   Map 3
Arados   129
Aram-naharaim   64, Map 2
Araunah   93, 94, Map 4
Arbela   EP
Archelaus   152, 153
Aretas IV, King   *138 f*★
Arimathea   Map 8
Aristobulus   135, 139

Ark of the Covenant 86, 92, 93
Armenia 16, Map 7
Arnon 25, 79, *78 t*, Maps 1, 5
Aroer Maps 3, 5
Arpad Map 6
Arqa Map 2
Arslân-Tash 53 *★, 101★*, EP
Artemis 170, *174 t*
Arubboth Map 5
Arumah Map 3
Arvad 16, 51, 129, *18 t, 40 t*, Map 2
Asa 116
Ashdod Maps 1, 3, 5, 6, 8
Asher Map 3
Ashkelon 129, Maps 1, 3, 5, 8
Ashtaroth *113 f★*, Map 2
Ashur Maps 6, EP
Ashurbanipal 110, 116, *111★, 112 f★, 114★*
Ashurdan III 116
Ashurnasirpal 116
Ashur-nirari 116
Asia (province) Map 9
Asphalt Lake Map 9
Assos Map 9
Assuân 124, *131 f★*
Assyria 109, 110, Maps 6, EP
Assyrians 116, 135
Ataroth Map 5
Athaliah 116
Athens 135, 151, Maps 7, 9, EP
Aton 44
Attalia Map 9
Augustus 136, 152, 153
Azekah Maps 3, 5
Azariah 110
Azotus Map 8

B

Baal 99, 115, *53 f★*
Ba'albek 136, *139 t★*, Map 2
Baal-hazor 25, Map 1
Baal-meon Map 5
Baal-perazim 92
Baal-shalishah Map 5
Baal-shamem 130
Baal-zephon 74
Baasha 116
Babel, Tower of *125★*

Babylon 9, 16, 117, 123, 129, *125★*, Maps 6, 7, EP
Babylonia 124, Maps 6, 7, EP
Baghdad 16, EP
Bahr Lût *70★*
Bahurim *97 f★*
Baibars 31
Balîkh Map 2
Barak 52, 86, 159, Map 3
Barnabas Map 9
Baruch 123, *54★*
Bashan Map 1
Beeroth 118, Map 3
Beer-sheba Maps 1, 2, 3, 5, 8
Behistun 45, EP
Beirut EP
Beisân 52
Beit Sahûr *162★*
Beni-hasan *62★*, EP
Benjamin Map 3
Beqa' 10, 153, *139 t★*
Beroea Map 9
Berytus 129
Beth-anath Map 3
Bethany (nr. Jerusalem) 160, Map 8
Bethany (trans-Jordan) 159
Beth-arbel Map 5
Bethel 64, 85, 99, 118, Maps 3, 5
Bethesda Map 4
Beth-ezel Map 5
Beth-gamul Map 5
Beth-haggan Map 5
Beth-horon Maps 3, 5
Beth-jeshimoth Map 3
Bethlehem (in Judah) 52, 91, 151, *156, 162★*, Maps 1, 2, 3, 5, 8
Bethlehem (in Zebulun) Map 3
Bethphage *97 f★*
Beth-saida 160, Map 8
Beth-shan 26, 52, 94, 129, *41★, 53 f★, 89 f★*, Maps 1, 2, 5
Beth-shemesh Map 5
Beth-shittah Map 3
Beth-zatha Map 4
Beth-zur Map 5
Bezabde *17 f★*
Bezek Map 5
Bisutun 45, EP
Bithynia Map 9
Boghaz-Keui EP

Bozra Maps 2, 6
Brick-bakers 74, *75*
Busra Map 2
Byblos 15, 31, 129, *19★, 30★*, Maps 2, 6, 7

C

Caesarea 151, Maps 1, 8, 9
Caesarea Philippi 160, Map 8
Caiaphas' dwelling Map 4
Cairo EP
Calah *108★*, EP
Caligula 152, 153
Calno Map 6
Calvary 160, *97 t★*
Cambyses 116
Camel 9
Cana Map 8
Canaan 15, 51, 64, Map 2
Capernaum 160, Maps 1, 8
Carchemish Maps 2, 6, EP
Caria Map 9
Carmel, Mount 25, 79, 109, 115, 118, 159, *119*, Maps 1, 3, 5
Carmel (in Judah) Map 5
Cassius Longinus 152
Cauda Map 9
Cedars 15, 93, *13★, 14★*
Cenacle *97 t★*
Cenchreae Map 9
Cestius Gallus 152
Chalcis 153
Chaldaeans 116, 123, Map 6
Champollion, J. F. 43
Chephirah Map 3
Cherubim *101, 104★*
Chinnereth Maps 3, 5
Chios Map 9
Chnumhotep 64, *62★*
Chorazin 160, Map 8
Chronicles 58, 100
Chronicler 124
Cilicia 109, 169, Maps 6, 7, 9
Cilician Gates *173*
Cizre 16, *17 f★*, EP
Claudius 152, 153
Clay nails *48 t*
Cleopatra 136, *133 r★*
Cnidus Map 9
Coins *127★, 132t, 133l*
Colossae Map 9

Colossians 170
Colossians, Epistle to the
152, Map 9
Commodus 132 t★
Coponius 152
Corbulo 152
Corinth 172 tr, Map 9
Corinthians, Epistles to the
152, Map 9
Cos Map 9
Crete 86, Maps 6, 7, 9
Cuneiform writing 45, 47★
Cuspius Fadus 152
Cyprus 16, 98 f★, Maps, 9
EP
Cyrene EP
Cyrus 116, 124, EP

D

Dalmanutha 160
Damascus 109, 129, 151,
170, Maps 2, 6, 7, EP
Dan 99, Maps 1, 2, 5
Daniel (book) 130, 127 t★
Darius I 45, 116, 126 t★
David 46, 63, 91 4, 99, 116,
135, 151
Dead, Book of the 44, 55 t★
Dead Sea 9, 25, 64, 135,
145, 146, 24★, 70★, Maps 1,
8
Debir Map 3
Deborah 86, Map 3
Decapolis Map 8
Delta of the Nile 15, 64, 73
Denderah 133 r★, EP
Deportation policy 110, 117
Derbe Map 9
Deutero-Isaiah 116, 117,
123
Deuteronomy 79
Diadochi 129
Diana Map 9
Diaspora (Dispersion) 124,
169
Dibon 37, 171 f★, Maps 1, 5
Dispersion 124, 169
Dominus Flevit 41 f★, 97★,
Map 4
Domitian 152
Dor Maps 2, 3, 5
Dothan 37, 35★, Maps 1,
2, 5
Dur Sharrukīn 110, 112 t★

E

Ebal 25, Map 3
Ecbatana Maps 7, EP
Ecclesiastes 130, 95 f★
Ecclesiasticus 130
Edfu 31, 132 f★
Edom 64, 109, Map 6
Edomites 63, 151, 28 f★
Edrei Map 2
Eglon 52
Egypt 15, 16, Maps 6, EP
Ehud 86, Map 3
Ekron 52, Maps 1, 5
Elah 116
El-Amarna 44, 51, EP
Elam Map 5
Elamites 45
Elath 9, 93, Map 6
El:Balu'a 53 f★
Elealeh Map 5
Elephantine 31, 124, 131★
Elijah 109, 110, 116, 159
Elisha 109, 115, 116
El-Jīb 52, 82 c★
El-Muqanna' 52
Eltekeh 52
Emmaa Map 7
Emmaus Map 8
En-dor 89 f★, Map 5
En-gedi Map 5
En-rogel Map 4
Entemena 48 t★
Ephesians, Epistle to the
152
Ephesus 170, Maps 7, 9, EP
Ephraim 25, 99, Maps 1, 3
Ephron Map 5
Erech 48 t★, EP
Esarhaddon 116, Map 6
Esau 63
Esdraelon 158 f★
Eshtaol Map 3
Eshtemoa Map 5
Essenes 145, 146
Esther (book) 124
Etham Map 5
Ethnarch 153
Et-Tell 85
Euphrates 16, 118, 17 t★,
125★, Maps 2, 7, EP
Eusebius 52
Evil-merodach 116
Excavation 37, 38
Ezekiel 116, 117, 123
Ezion-geber 10, 93

Ezra 116, 124
Ezra (book) 58, 127 t★

F

Fair Havens Map 9
Fashkha Spring 146
Felix, Antonius 152, Map 9
Festus, Porcius 152, Map 9
Flinders Petrie, W. 37
Forum of Appius Map 9

G

Gabbatha 160, Map 4
Gad 116
Gadara Map 8
Galatia 170, Map 9
Galatians (book) 152,
Map 9
Galba 152
Galilee 159, Maps 1, 8
Galilee, Sea of 9, 159, 164–
165, Map 1
Gallim 118
Gallio Map 9
Gamaliel 169
Gath Map0 3, 5
Gath-hepher Map 5
Gaugamela 17 f★, Map 7
Gaulanitis Map 8
Gaza 37, 129, Maps 1, 2, 3,
5, 7, 8,
Geba 86, 118, 88★, Maps 1, 5
Gebal 31, Map 2
Gebim 118
Gehenna Map 4
Ge-hinnom Map 4
Gennesaret, Lake of Map 8
Gerar Maps 2, 5
Gerasa Maps 1, 8
Gerizim, Mount 25, 67 f,
68–69, Maps 3, 8
Geshur Map 5
Gessius Florus 152
Gethsemane, Garden of 160,
97★, Map 4
Gezer 37, 92, Maps 1, 2, 3, 5
Gibbethon Map 5
Gibeah 118, Maps 3, 5
Gibeon 26, 52, 79, 92, 118,
53 t★, 81★, 82 c, 106 t★
Maps 1, 3, 5
Giblet 31
Gideon 86, Map 3

191

Gihon, Spring   92, *97 t*★,
    106 f★, Map 4
Gilboa 25, 86, 91, 159, *89 f*,
    Maps 1, 5
Gilead   109, Map 1
Gilgal (in Ephraim) Map 5
Gilgal (in Benjamin)   86,
    Maps 3, 5
Gimzo   Map 5
Gobryas   *48 c*★
Golgotha   Map 4
Gomorrah   Map 2
Gordium   Map 7
Goshen, Land of   74
Gospels   153, 154
Gozan   Map 6
Gozarta   *17 f*★
Grotefend   45
Gubla   31

H

Habor   16
Hadad   *53 f*★
Hadadezer   109
Haggai   116, 117, 124
Haifa   118, *119*★, Map 1
Ham   15, Map 2
Hamanu   *111*★
Hamath (*Hama*) 32, 109, *33*,
    Maps 2, 6, EP
Hammurabi 45, *17 t*★, *47 t*★
Hannibal   135
Haran (*Harrân*) 64, *61 t*★,
    Maps 2, 6, EP
Harosheth-ha-goiim Map 3
Harp player   *95 f*★
Hasmonaeans 135, 136, 151,
    Map 4
Hathor   *133 r*★
Hatshepsut   44, 91,
    23 f★, *95 t*★
Hattushash   EP
Hazael   *101*★
Hazazon-tamar   Map 2
Hazor 37, 79, 85, 93, 99,
    83★, *98 t*★, *103*★, Maps 1,
    2, 3, 5
Hebrews   74
Hebron 25, 64, 91, 151,
    157 f, Maps 1, 2, 3, 5
Hecatompylos   Map 7
Heliodorus   135
Helios   *139 t*★
Hepher   Maps 3, 5

Hermon, Mount 10, 79, 160,
    12 f, Map 2
Herod Antipas   152, 153,
    159
Herod the Great   93, 136,
    151, 152
Herodium   151, *34 f*, *162*★,
    Map 8
Heshbon   52, Maps 3, 5
Hezekiah   92, 100, 116,
    106 f★
Hieratic script   44
Hieroglyphs   43
Highways   26
Hill Country   Map 3
Hinnom, Valley of   Map 4
Hippos   Map 8
Hittites   16, 46, 73, *50*★,
    EP
Hophra (Apries)   116
Horemheb   73, *72*★
Horus   44, *132 f*★
Hosea (prophet)   116, 117
Hoshea (Joshua)   85
Hoshea (king of Israel) 116
Huldah   116
Huleh, Lake   Map 1
Hyksos   73
Hyrcanium   151, *34 c*
Hyrcanus, John   135, 136,
    146

I

Ibleam   Map 5
Ibsha   73, *62*★
Iconium   Map 9
Idols   *89 t*
Idumaea   Map 8
Idumaeans   135
Ilium   Map 7
India   129
Iran   16
Irpeel   118
Isaiah 64, 99, 116, 117, 118,
    135, *114*★
Ishmael   86
Ishtar   110
Israel   99, 100
Issachar   Map 3
Issus   129, Map 7
Islanbul   EP
Ituraeans   135
Ivory carving   *101*

J

Jabbok   25, 64, *11*★, *66 f*,
    Maps 1, 5
Jabesh-gilead   Maps 3, 5
Jabneel   Map 5
Jacob   63, 73, 99
Jacob's Well   *67 f*, *68–69*★,
    Map 8
Jaffa   Map 1
Jahaz   Map 3
Jamnia   Map 8
Jarmuth   Map 3
Jattir   Map 5
Jazer   Map 5
Jeba‘   *88 t*★
Jebeil   31, *30*★
Jebel Mûsa   *76 f*★
Jehoahaz   116
Jehoiachin   116
Jehoiakim   116
Jehoshaphat   116
Jehu, King   109, 116, *108*★
Jehud   *127 t*★
Jephthah   86, Map 3
Jeremiah 115, 116, 117, 118,
    123, *54*★
Jericho 37, 85, *82 t*★, Maps
    1, 2, 3, 5, 8
Jeroboam I   99, 116
Jeroboam II   110, 116, 117
Jerusalem   52, 91–4, *97*★,
    Maps 1–9, EP
Jesanah   Map 5
Jesus of Nazareth 124, 147,
    153f., 159f., 169f.
Jezîret Ibn Omar   *17 f*★
Jezreel   *89 f*★, Map 5
Jezreel, Plain of 25, 26, 159,
    158 f★, Map 1
Joahaz   116
Joash   116
Job (book)   124
Joel (book)   124
John (Gospel and Epistles)
    152, 154
John the Baptist 152, 159,
    60 t★
Jokneam   Maps 3, 5
Jonah   116, 124
Jonathan Maccabaeus 130,
    135, 145
Joppa   129, Maps 2, 5, 8
Joram   116
Jordan (river and valley) 9f.,
    79, *11*★, *161*★, Maps 1, 8

Joseph 73
Joseph of Arimathea Map 4
Josephus, Flavius 135, 145, 146, 152, 159
Joshua 79 f., 85, Map 3
Joshua (book) 58, 79
Josiah 79, 85, 100, 116, 117, 123, 135
Jotham 116
Judaea Map 8
Judah 80, 99, 100, Maps 1, 3
Judas Maccabaeus 130
Judges 86
Judges (book) 58, 86
Julias 160, Map 8
Jupiter 139 t★
Justinian 77★

K

Kabul Map 5
Kadesh 74, 79
Kadesh (on the Orontes) Map 2
Kafr Kenna 25, 27 t, 155, Map 8
Kaftor 86
Kamon Map 3
Karnak 31, 22 f★, EP
Kedesh Maps 3, 5
Kenyon, Miss K. 85
Khâbûr 16, 46
Khirbet Qumrân 37, 145 f., 59★, 60★, 140-4★, 147-9★, Maps 1, 8
Khorsabad 110, Maps 6, EP
Kidron Valley 93, 160, 29 f, 96 t, 97★, 166 f, Map 4
Kings 58, 100
Kir-hareseth Map 5
Kiriathaim, Plain of Map 2
Kiriath-jearim 92, Map 3
Kir-moab Map 5
Koinè Greek 170

L

Lachish 52, 79, 85, 123, 54★ 82 f, Maps 1, 3, 5
Lagash 16, 48 t★, EP
Laishah 118
Laodicea Map 9
Laisa EP
Lasea Map 9

Law, The 57, 124, 145
Lebanon 10, 31, 93, Map 2
Lebo-hamath Map 2
Lebonah Map 3
Leviticus 124
Libnah Map 3, 5
Lithostroton Map 4
Lot 64, 70★
Lowland 26, Map 3
Luke 152, 154, 169
Luxor 31, 22 f★, 71★, EP
Lycaonia Map 9
Lycia Map 9
Lydda Map 8
Lydia Map 9
Lysanias 153
Lystra Map 9

M

Maat 44
Maccabees 130, 135
Macedonia Maps 7, 9, EP
Machaerus 151, 159, 34 t, Map 8
Madaba 171 f★
Madmenah 118
Madon Map 3
Magadan 160
Magdala Map 8
Magnesia 135, EP
Mahanaim Maps 2, 5
Makaz Map 5
Makkedah Map 3
Malachi 124
Malta Map 9
Manasseh (tribe) 99
Manasseh (King of Judah) 116
Maon Map 5
Marcellus 152
Marduk 123 f.
Mareshah Map 5
Mari 17 t, 83 t★, EP
Mark (Gospel) 152, 154
Mark 154, Map 9
Mar Saba 29 f★, Map 8
Marullus 152
Masada 151, Map 8
Matthew (Gospel) 152, 154
Matthew 154
Medeba 171 t★, Map 5
Medes 130, Map 6
Media Map 7
Megiddo 26, 37, 92-3, 84 t,

98 f, 102 f, 104★, Maps 1, 2, 3, 5
Mekal 53 f★
Melchizedek 94
Memphis 15, 31, 73, 20-21, Maps 6, 7, EP
Menahem 116
Mendes 129
Menes 15
Mephaath Map 5
Merom 79, Map 3
Meroz Map 3
Mesha 109
Mesopotamia 16, 31, 135, Map 7
Messiah 93, 154
Micah 116
Michmash 86, 118, 88★
Middle Kingdom 46
Migdol 74
Migron 118
Miletus Maps 7, 9
Minet el-Beida 51
Minnith Map 3
Misrephoth-maim Map 3
Mitanni 46, 50★
Mizpah 118, 107 t★, Maps 1, 3, 5
Mizpah of Gilead Maps 2, 3
Moab 64, 79, 86, 109, 53 f★, Maps 1, 3, 5
Moph 20-21
Moreh, Hill of Map 3
Moresheth Map 5
Moses 57, 74, 79, 85, 118
Mount of Offence 96 t★, Map 4
Mount of Olives 118, 160, Map 4
Mucianus 152
Mukhmâs 88 t★
Mycenaean pottery 39★
Myra Map 9
Mysia Map 9

N

Nabataeans 136, Map 8
Nabonidus 116
Nabopolassar 116
Nabuchodonosor 48 c★
Nadab 116
Nag Hammadi EP
Nahor 86
Nahum 116

Nain   89 f★, Map 8
Nathan   92, 93, 115, 116
Naucratis   129
Nazareth   25, 159, 158 f,
                Maps 1, 8
Neapolis   Map 9
Nebi Samwîl   26, 82 c★
Nebo, Mount   79, 78 f
Nebuchadnezzar 116, 123,
                48 c★, 125★
Necho   116
Negeb   64, 28 f★, Map 2
Nehemiah   116, 124
Nehemiah (book) 58, 124
Nephtoah   118
Nergal-sharezer 116, 48 c★
Nero   152, 153
Nerva   152
Netophah   Map 5
New Kingdom   46
Nile   15f., 22, 131 f, EP
Nimrûd   108★
Nineveh 111★, Maps 6, EP
Nippur   16, EP
No-Amon   22 f★
Nob   118, 97 f★
Nomads   66 t★
Noph   20–21
Nuzi   EP

O

Obadiah   124
Obelisks   43, 110, 19, 42
Octavian   136
Oil lamps   38, 39★
Old Kingdom   46
Omri 100, 109, 116, 105 f★,
                108★
Ophel   Map 4
Opis   Map 7
Ornan (Araunah) 93, 94,
                Map 4
Orontes 10, 32, 129, 33 f,
                Map 2
Osiris   44
Ossuaria 41 f, 167f★, 168 t★
Ostraca   54★

P

Paddan-aram   64
Palmyra   136, 137, 139 f,
                Map 7
Pamphylia   Map 9
Paneion   129

Paphos   Map 9
Papyrus   32, 44, 124
Parables   159
Parah   118, 120 f
Parthia   Map 7
Parthians   136, 146
Patara   Map 9
Patenemheb   95 f★
Patriarchs   63 f.
Paul, St   152, 154, 169 f.
                Map 9,
Pavement, the   160, Map 4
Pekah   116
Pekahiah   116
Pella (in Palestine) Maps 2,
                8
Pella (in Macedonia) Map 7
Pelusium   74, 129
Peniel   64
Pentateuch   57, 58, 63, 80
Penuel or Peniel   26, 64,
                Maps 1, 2, 3, 5
Peraea   160, Map 8
Perath   118
Perga   Map 9
Pergamum   Maps 7, 9
Persepolis   45, 124, 129,
                126, Map 7
Persia   EP
Persians   116
Peter   152, 154, 160, 170
Pethor   Map 2
Petra   10, 136, 138★
Petronius   152
Pharisees   135 f., 160
Pharos   129, 132 tl
Philadelphia   129, 130,
                Map 8
Philadelphia (in Asia)
                Map 9
Philemon   Map 9
Philemon (Epistle) 152
Philip (tetrarch) 152, 153,
                160
Philippi   Map 9
Philippians, Epistle to the
                152, Map 9
Philistia   Map 1
Philistines   86, 91 f., 87,
                Maps 3, 5
Philo   145, 146
Phoenix   Map 9
Phylactery   60 fr★
Pi-hahiroth   74
Pirathon   Maps 3, 5
Pisidia   Map 9

Plain, Sea of the 24★, Map 5
Pliny   145
Pompey   136
Pontius Pilate 152
Pontus   Map 9
Popilius Laenas 135
Pottery   38, 39★
Praetorium   Map 4
Prophets   115, 117 f.
Psalms   124
Ptolemais   129, 130, Maps
                8, 9
Ptolemies 129 f., 135, EP
Ptolemy I   128 f
Ptolemy II   132 t★
Ptolemy III   133l★
Ptolemy VI   133l★
Punon   Map 2
Puteoli   Map 9
Pyramids   38

Q

Qarqar   100, 109, 116,
                Maps 2, 6
Qatna   Map 2
Quintilius Varus 152
Quirinius   152
Qumrân, see Khirbet Qumrân

R

Rabbah of the Ammonites
                129, 130, Map 5
Ramah   118, Map 5
Ramathaim   Map 5
Rameses II   73, 50★, 71★
Rameses III   86, 87★
Ramoth-gilead 109,   Maps
                1, 5
Raphia   129
Râs Shamra   16, 51, Map 2
Rawlinson, Sir Henry   45
Red Sea 10, 73 f., 79, EP
Reeds, Sea of   74
Rehob   Map 3
Rehoboam   100, 116
Rehoboth   Map 2
Rekhmire   74
Rephaim, Valley of Map 4
Retenu   90 f★
Revelation (book) 152
Rezeph   Map 6
Rhegium   Map 9
Rhodes   151, Maps 9, EP
Rimmon   Map 3

Rogelim Map 5
Romans, Epistle to the
152, Map 9
Rome 135, 136, Map 9
Ruâd 18 t

S

Sadducees 135 f. 145
St Catherine, monastery of
74, 77*
Sais 129, Map 6
Salamis (on Cyprus) Map 9
Salecah Map 2
Salim 159, Map 8
Salt Sea 24*, Maps 2, 5
Samaria 26, 37, 100, 129,
151, 160, 54*, 105 f, 157 t*,
Maps 1, 5, 6, 8, EP
Samos Map 9
Samothrace Map 9
Samson 86, Map 3
Samuel 58, 86, 91
Sanhedrin Map 4
Saphon 51
Sarcophagus 41 r*
Sardis Maps 7, 9
Sargon II 110, 116, 112 t*,
Map 6
Saul 86, 91, 115
Scarab seals 54*
Scipio Africanus 135
Scythopolis 129, Map 8
Seals 49*, 54*
Sebaste 151, 105 f*, Map 8
Sebastiyeh 105 f*
Seh 63
Sela 138 f*
Seleucia Map 9
Seleucids 129 f., 135,
172 f*, EP
Seleucus IV 135
Sennacherib 99, 110, 116,
117, Map 6
Sergius Paulus Map 9
Sesostris II 62*
Set 51
Seti I 14*
Sewêne 124
Shallum 116
Shalmaneser III 109, 116,
108*
Shalmaneser IV 116
Shalmaneser V 100, 110,
116
Shamshi-adad 116

Sharon, Plain of 25, Maps
1, 3, 8
Sharuhen Map 2
Shechem 25, 26, 37, 64,
99, 160, 67 f, 68–69, Maps
1, 2, 3, 5
Shema 60 r*
Sheshbazzar 116, 124
Shiloh 86, 99, Maps 1, 3, 5
Shimron Map 3
Shishak (Sheshonq) 100,
116
Shulgi 48 f*
Shunem 89 f*, Map 5
Siddim, Valley of Map 2
Sidon 129, 160, Maps 2,
7, 9
Silas Map 9
Siloam, pool of Map 4
Siloam, tower of Map 4
Silwân 96 t*
Simon Maccabaeus 130
Sin Map 2
Sinai 10, 74, 76 f, EP
Sirach 130
Smyrna 135, Maps 9, EP
Socoh Map 5
Sodom Map 2
Solomon 92–4, 99, 116
Stelae 109, 53 f*
Stephen 152
Street called Straight
172 tl*
Succoth 64, 67 t, Maps 2,
3, 5
Sultantepe 61 t*, Map 1
Sumer 45, EP
Susa 124, Maps 6, 7, EP
Sychar Map 8
Syene 124
Syracuse Map 9
Syria Maps 7, 9
Syrian desert 9, EP
Syro-Arabian desert 9,
Map 2
Syro-Phoenicia Map 8
Syrtis Map 9

T

Taanach 37, 52, Maps 1, 2,
5
Tabor, Mount 86, 159, 160,
27 f, 84, Maps 1, 3, 8
Talmud 159

Tanis 129
Tappuah (in Ephraim)
Maps 3, 5
Tarsus 169, Maps 2, 9, EP
Taurus Maps 2, 7
Tekoa 117, Map 5
Teleilât el-Ghassûl Map 1
Tell 32, 37 f.
Tell Abu Hawâm Map 1
Tell Beit Mirsim 85, Map 1
Tell Deir 'Alla 67 t*
Tell ed-Dâmiyeh 11*
Tell el-'Ajjûl 41 c*, Map 1
Tell ed-Duweir 52
Tell el-Fâra'ah Map 1
Tell el-Hesy 37, 52, Map 1
Tell el-Hosn 52
Tell el-Qasîleh 54*, Map 1
Tell en-Nasbeh 107 t*
Tell Jemmeh Map 1
Tell Ta'anak 52
Tell Waqqâs 83 t*
Temple (of Herod) 151
Temple (of Solomon) 102 t,
103*
Temple square 166 t
Tetragram 59*
Tetrarch 153
Thapsacus Map 7
Thebes 15, 43, 22 f, EP
Thebez Maps 3, 5
Thessalonica 170, Map 9
Thessalonians, Epistle to
the 116
Thoth 44
Thothmes III 44, 51, 52,
91, 83 t*, 90 t*
Thrace Maps 7, 9
Three Taverns Map 9
Thyatira Map 9
Tiberias 159, 164–165,
Map 8
Tiberius 152, 159
Tiberius Alexander 152
Tiglath-pileser III 110, 116,
117, 113t*, Map 6
Tigris 16, 17 f, Maps 7, EP
Timnah Map 3
Timnath-serah Map 3
Timothy Map 9
Timothy, Epistles to 152
Tirhakah 116
Tirzah 25, 26, 37, 100, 109,
36, 105 t, Maps 1, 2, 3, 5
Tishbe Map 5
Titus, Epistle to 152, 170

Titus, Arch of   *174 f* ★
Trajan   152
Tripolis   10, 31, 129, *12 t*
Troas   Map 9
Tribes of Israel   86
Tutankhamon 81, *72*★, *90*★
Tyre   109, 110, 129, 151,
  160, *18 f*, Maps 2, 5, 6, 7, 9
Tyropoeon Valley   *97*★

U

Ugarit   16, 51, Map 2
Ummidius Quadratus   152
Unger, E.   *125*★
Ur 16, 64, *48 f*★, *61c*, Maps
  6, EP
Uriah (prophet)   115, 116
Uruk   *48 t*★
Uzziah (Azariah)
    110, 116, 117

V

Valerius Gratus   152
Valley of the Kings   *23 t*★
Ventidius Cumanus   152
Vespasian   152

Vibius Marsius   152
Vitellius   152
Volusius Saturninus   152

W

Wâdi Farʿah   *11*★
Wâdi Murabaʿat   *60 r*
Water tunnels   92, *106*,
    107 f, Map 4
Wilderness of Judah (Ju-
  daea)   26, 159, *29, 162*,
    Map 1
Winnowing   118, *121 f*
Writing prophets 116, 117 f.

X

Xerxes   *126 t*★
Xystos   Map 4

Y

Yahweh   80, 94, 99, *59 f*
Yahwism   118
Yahwistic chronicle   94

Yahwistic history   124
Yarmuk   25, Map 1

Z

Zab, Great   16
Zab, Little   16
Zaphon   51
Zarephath   Map 2
Zebedee   160
Zeboim   Map 2
Zebulun   Map 3
Zechariah   116, 117, 124
Zedekiah   116
Zemar   51, Map 2
Zemarites   51
Zephaniah   116
Zered, Brook   *65 t*★
Zeredah   Map 5
Zerubbabel   116, 124
Zeus   130, *133 l*★
Ziggurats   31, *49*★, *61*★,
    112 t★, *125*★
Zion   92, 93, Map 4
Ziph   Map 5
Zimri   116
Zoar   Map 2
Zorah   Maps 3, 5
Zoser   *20–21*

Printed in the Netherlands by
N.V. Drukkerij Hooiberg, Epe.